GW00456530

Network Marketeers...

Target Success!

The Complete Planner For Your First Year In Business

David Barber

Insight Network Marketing Library

InSIGHT
PUBLISHING

Network Marketeers... Target Success!
David Barber

Insight Publishing Ltd
Sterling House
Church Street
Ross-on-Wye
Herefordshire
HR9 5HN

Phone: 01989-564496
Fax: 01989-565596

© David Barber 1996

The right of David Barber to be identified as the author of this work has been asserted by him in accordance with the Copyright, Designs and Patents Act 1988.

All rights reserved. For information, contact Insight Publishing.

Making copies from this book

You are welcome to copy the tables at the back of this book for your own use. You may also copy them for free distribution to your downlines. However we ask you to respect the author's copyright and refrain from copying the text, and in particular, to refrain from *selling* copies of any part of the book.

Notice of Liability

While great care has been taken in the preparation of this publication, it should not be used as a substitute for appropriate professional advice. Neither the author nor Insight Publishing can accept any liability for loss or damage occasioned by any person acting as a result of the material in this book.

Acknowledgement

The Business Activity Agreement (BACTA) has been developed from an idea originally discussed with Martin Kern. Many distributors have used the idea with great success, and I, and they, are greatly indebted to Martin.

ISBN: 1-899298-07-X

Cover design by James Hutcheson Design, Edinburgh
Printed in Finland by WSOY

Contents

Forms

Diagrams & Exercises

Introduction

A few years ago I had the good fortune to become involved in network marketing. However, I nearly dropped out before I had really even started. My reasons were the same as those of so many others: I failed to understand the business and treat it as the deadly serious opportunity that it is; I failed to write a Contact List; I did not set any goals; I failed to make a plan of action to help me succeed.

Fortunately, I made a commitment to learn everything I possibly could about the company, the products and the business method itself. Having devoured every book, audio tape and video I could find and attended every available training, I gained a basic understanding and went to work.

Within six months I had built a rapidly expanding group of some six hundred distributors spanning several countries. With this growth came a new challenge. I was still part-time and unable to meet personally with all of the new members in my group. I needed a way to help new distributors get off on the right footing: to teach them to understand the industry, how to set goals, how to write a Contact List and how to plan the growth of their business.

The answer was a workbook called *Frogfishing* and it proved tremendously successful—so much so that requests poured in from distributors in other companies to personalise it for them. I had no time to take this on, but I had struck up a friendship with David Barber, who was preparing the superb *S.T.A.R. Leadership Programme*. By coincidence, he was looking for a workbook to compliment his *S.T.A.R.* books and took on the task of re-writing *Frogfishing* in a form that would be valuable to distributors and groups in any company.

Although retaining the basic philosophy behind *Frogfishing*, David has refined and expanded the concept to create a superb product for **you** the independent distributor. *TARGET SUCCESS!*, especially when used in conjunction with David's *S.T.A.R. Leadership Programme*, will show you how to treat your business seriously, set goals and plan your business. Just as with any other field of business, in network marketing success will always be the result of following a plan.

I truly believe that if you make a commitment to learn everything there is to learn about your business and commit yourself to sticking with it for at least one year, if you become a student of your own personal potential and learn how to develop the right attitude toward yourself and others, and if you follow this workbook and the *S.T.A.R. Leadership Programme*, you will not only reap massive financial dividends but also grow in stature as a human being. This is one of the remarkable spin-offs of network marketing. Success is as much about the journey as it is about the destination. While it has to begin with deciding upon your destination, it must then be accompanied by a plan to take you there.

Remember that those who fail to plan are planning to fail.

Wishing you all the best with your business

—*Russell Webster*

> **Author's Note**: *TARGET SUCCESS!* can be used as a 'stand-alone' tool in its own right, or with the training scheme of your company or your group, or you can use it with the *S.T.A.R. Leadership Programme*. (If you wish to use it in the latter way, the books in the Programme to which you should refer are shown on page 93)

Unless You PLAN For Success, You Cannot Make It Happen

SUCCESS COMES FROM TARGETED ACTION

A Catherine wheel looks and sounds terrific as it *whooshes*, spins and showers sparks in all directions. But despite all its power, it is going nowhere—all it is doing is chasing it's tail. Just like the Catherine wheel, any action which does not contribute directly to achieving what you want is *wasted* action.

Emulate instead the rocket, aiming unerringly at its target.

How do you emulate a rocket? First, know exactly what your target is, otherwise you cannot aim for it. And the more clearly and sharply you can see your target, the more likely you are to hit it. Second, direct your actions to aim straight for your target. This is what *TARGET SUCCESS!* is all about.

In network marketing, this means that your actions should be focused, in correct proportion, *only* on **The Four Must-do Activities For Success**:

- Sponsoring
- Retailing
- Teaching
- Applying Winning Attitudes to each of the above.

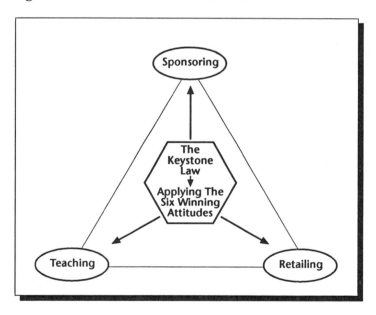

Sponsoring, Retailing and Teaching form the outer triangle because these are the three activities you do with other people. Winning Attitudes are placed in the centre for two reasons: because they are an inner activity, a question of inner development; and because they are the driving force behind the other three.

*Your **Attitudes** determine **precisely** how great, or poor, your success will be*

The Winning Attitudes are in turn driven by **The Keystone Law,** the fundamental truth about network marketing which will be the key to your success:

*Your path to success is **ONLY** through your people*

5

There is no secret to building a successful network marketing business. Every **proven** distributor in every network has done it in the same way, through these four Must-Do Activities of:

- Showing the opportunity as simply as possible
- Showing the products as simply as possible
- Teaching others to do the same in the simplest possible way; *and*
- Applying Winning Attitudes to these activities.

Nothing else earns you anything, so don't do it!

Do enough of each, teach your people to do the same, and you will succeed.

But you also have to do each in **correct proportion** to the others. The easiest way to keep your actions focused is to write down **what** you have to do, and **when**, to achieve what you want. *TARGET SUCCESS!* will help you to do this.

The quickest, easiest way to success is to have a clear, written plan—*and then follow it*

FAILING TO PLAN MEANS PLANNING TO FAIL

PLANNING WILL HELP YOU TO STAY ON-TRACK

Staying On-Track means:

- Putting in the time and effort required to achieve your goals in the business
- Learning how to work the business in the right way, *and*
- Applying what you have learned consistently and with the right attitudes.

Failure is commonly caused by Going Off-Track through over-complicating the business or not sticking to the proven way of doing things. If you want to make the most of the wonderful opportunity offered by this great industry of ours, you must learn the simple, proven ways of working the business and then *stick to them consistently*. The planning method you will learn in *TARGET SUCCESS!* is the best way to ensure that you and your people Stay On-Track.

HOW *TARGET SUCCESS!* CAN HELP YOU MANAGE YOUR BUSINESS

TARGET SUCCESS! is also an important management tool. It shows you:

- All the steps you must follow as you build your business
- All the steps you should train your downlines to follow
- All the administrative back-up systems you need for the whole of your first year so that:
  - You know **at any time** how well you and your group are doing
  - You know at any time **what** your downline leaders should be doing to help you to achieve the targets you want
  - You have an **immediate** warning system should anything go wrong, *and*
  - You know **at all times** with whom you should be working in your group.
- Easy ways to keep track of your money. Although boring for most of us, you really do need to keep track of your financial affairs. *TARGET SUCCESS!* shows you the simplest, most painless way to do this
- What you need to buy to set up your business.

How Do You Create A Pathway To Success?

PLANS, BY THEMSELVES, ACHIEVE NOTHING

Although it is essential to your success, planning by itself makes nothing happen. Writing down your goals does not mean that you will achieve them—if wishes were horses, beggars would ride and none of us would ever want for anything in our lives. No, plans and goals have only one purpose: to point you in the right direction.

In *every* field of human endeavour, and network marketing is no different, it is **ACTION** plus **ATTITUDE** plus **KNOWLEDGE** which will bring you success.

- ACTION means doing as much as you possibly can of whatever is necessary.

- ATTITUDE means bringing a sense of: Urgency, Excitement, Conviction *and* Determination to your actions.

- KNOWLEDGE determines how well you *can* act whereas attitudes decide how well you *will* act.

If you are not going to apply what you learn to your actions,
don't waste valuable time learning it

YOUR GOALS ARE YOUR GREAT MOTIVATING POWER

The strength of your goals will determine the power of your actions.

It is what you aim for, and how badly you want it, which decides what you do *now*. It is your *goals* which both create the motivation to act and give you the attitude needed to make your actions successful. They do this by fuelling the **Bulldozer Mentality** and creating the **Desire** you need to achieve success.

*The stronger your Desire, the more **certain** your success.*
*The stronger your Desire, the **greater** your success.*
*Maximum success is impossible without **Burning Desire**.*
The strength of your Desire is set by the clarity and the desirability of your goals.

Research undertaken by Yale Business School found that the 3% of people who had clearly defined goals *earned more than the other 97% put together!*

Do you want to be one of the 3% or one of the 97%?

If previous attempts at goal-setting have not worked for you, it was because either you did not apply the concept properly or you did not find goals which really *excited* you, which really 'turned you on'. Might you have chosen, not the goals which you wanted for yourself, but the goals which your spouse, children, parents or peers wanted of you? Because many surveys have now proved that the *only* common factor among *all* successful people was that they set personal goals:

- They knew exactly what they wanted from life

- They reminded themselves *constantly* of those goals, *and*

- Their clear goals and constant reminders kept them working for those goals.

HOW TO SET YOUR GOALS

As you complete the form opposite, don't limit yourself to what you think you can reasonably expect to achieve or can reasonably afford, because this may mean that you do not find the goals which really *excite* you—and it is *only* these which will give you the motivation you need. Things you would 'quite like' are nowhere near desirable enough to generate the drive you will need to succeed.

Make your goals as *crystal-clear* as you can. Woolly ideas of what you would like are not enough. If you'd quite like a glass of wine, almost anything will do but, if you are desperate for a particular fine vintage, you will drive miles to get it! You need the clearest possible mental image of what you want for the mind to latch onto, before the mind will turn your goals into the powerful magnet you want them to be. How clearly can you taste, smell, see that special wine? So get to be able to 'touch, taste, smell and feel' your goals!

As you set your goals, don't forget your personal relationships! Many drop-outs are caused by the spouse not being 'on side'. In fact, I can think of almost no men who have succeeded in the teeth of apathy from their spouse. Although women cope better, even they rarely succeed if their spouse is unsympathetic to their aims. For most of us, a good intimate personal relationship is perhaps the most empowering force for success, happiness and fulfilment whereas a poor one can have the most undermining effect on our lives. So including your personal relationships in your goals can have a dramatic effect.

Write down your goals and contemplate them as often as you can. Once a day, as so many books and speakers tell you to do, is not enough. But don't just read them because that will achieve nothing. For this technique to work for you, you must imagine *vividly* how you would feel if you had achieved that goal—now!

*Feeling **now** the way you **will** feel when you have achieved your goals is the key.*

But you must also see your goals as something you have achieved *now* because, if you see them as in the future, that is where they will stay—in the future.

The purpose of goals is to make you *feel* in a particular way, so make sure you phrase them and see them not as something you are escaping from, but as something you are aiming towards. The subconscious mind is very literal.

For instance, if your aim is to avoid insecurity, your mind will concentrate on the word 'insecurity' and you will feel the lack and poverty which go with it. Concentrate instead on how having achieved your goals makes you feel good. You want to fill your being with positive feelings like 'plenty' and 'abundance' when you are reading and feeling your goals.

Finally, teach your people the value of *proper* goal-setting! If goals will be your great motivating power, can they not also be the great motivating power of your people?

ACQUIRE THE RIGHT KNOWLEDGE

Knowledge means that the more you know about *what* you should be doing, *how* you should be doing it and *why* you should be doing it, the more successful your actions will be—provided you *apply* that learning to your actions.

The best option is to find an experienced upline to work closely with you and your people until you feel confident enough to take over, but don't let it stop you if you cannot!

Goal Setting Exercise:
What Is Your Perfect Week?

Assuming you won a major lottery tomorrow, so that money was no object, how would you spend your perfect week?

*What would more money and time bring into your life that would really **excite** you, such as: relationships, possessions, leisure activities, special causes, and opportunities for education and self-development?*

*What would **excite** you enough to have you bounding out of bed each morning with eager anticipation?*

*Now write down the two or three of these goals which **most** excite you:*

*Finally, on a piece of card or paper, capture the essence of these goals in a way that really **excites** you: as a statement, a poem or an image. This is your Goals Sheet. Carry it with you everywhere, to review many times each day.*

Repeat this goal setting exercise every few months: as you develop in your business, you may soon outgrow your initial goals.

Although it is harder, plenty of people have succeeded without upline help. Whether you get help or not, apply the next three suggestions:

1. Build a library of books, tapes and videos on network marketing, your opportunity and personal development. This is an absolutely essential tool-kit!

2. Develop the Thirty-Minutes-A-Day Habit (see page 14)

3. Talk to *successful* distributors as much as you can. Go to as many meetings and trainings as you can. But *avoid unsuccessful distributors* because they blame the product, the company, network marketing, their sponsor—in fact, everyone and everything but themselves. You will have successful people and unsuccessful people in your company, yet *they all have exactly the same opportunity and exactly the same product!* So whose fault is it if someone is not making it work?

HOW MUCH HELP CAN YOU EXPECT FROM YOUR UPLINES?

Your uplines earn commission or royalty on your efforts, so this *entitles* you to expect their support! Having said that, certain well defined ways of doing things have, over the fifty-odd year history of network marketing, been proved to work; certain other actions have been proved, sooner or later, to lead to failure. Your uplines, from their own experience, will have found that if new distributors do not follow upline advice they rarely succeed. So, although your business belongs to you and you can run it in any way you like, you must also forgive your uplines if they choose not to work with you if you choose not to follow their advice.

The rule is that your uplines should only work as hard for you as you work for yourself. You can expect them to work *with* you, but don't expect them to work *instead of* you. For example, don't expect an upline to host a guest of yours at an opportunity meeting because you have a social engagement you 'can't get out of' or you can't get a baby-sitter. That is working *instead of*. But you can expect them to host a guest of yours at one opportunity meeting because you are taking a guest to another meeting in a different town, or you have a training session to attend or a Two-to-One to do, because that is Working *With* you and it is definitely in their interests to help you out!

WHICH DOWNLINES SHOULD YOU WORK WITH?

Give everyone the same and equal chance when they start, and then let them *self-select* into those who value your advice and act on it and those who do not. The best system is to work only with those who are prepared carry through all of the On-Track Landmarks (see page 13). Time spent with distributors who do not take your advice is time not spent with distributors who are working hard for you. Isn't it better for your business and fairer on those who do take your advice, to spend as much time as you can with them? So apply the same rules to your downlines as your uplines apply to you:

1. Work as hard for any of your people (but no harder) as they are prepared to work for themselves

2. Work *with* them, but not *instead of* them (see the examples above)

3. Do not work with any downline who is not prepared to Get On-Track and Stay On-Track (page 6).

If people are slow learners but are Staying On-Track, be patient with them: in time they may turn into 'golds' for you. If people Go Off-Track, your responsibility is discharged. Leave them to their own devices, but keep the door open for them to return on your terms.

BECOME A TEACHER—TEACH PLANNING FOR SUCCESS

Network marketing is a *teaching* business. Everything you learn, you must pass onto your people. Get *them* used to planning the *TARGET SUCCESS!* way, and *your* business will rocket to success!

Of the people who come into network marketing 90% fail, yet there is nothing exceptional about the 10% who succeed. They just understand that:

There is no point in doing anything unless they learn to do it properly.

What separates the 90% from the 10% is that the 10% take the trouble to find out how to do it, then just go ahead and do it.

Detailed planning is a vital part of focusing your people's actions on success. By planning your own work, you are giving your people a good example to follow. Those who copy your example will join the 10% and will succeed. How you plan your work (and what you should teach your people) is all covered in depth in the chapter *How To Target Your Actions On Success*, starting on page 19.

DEVELOP THE HABIT OF CONSISTENCY

Consistency means:

- Sticking to the plans and targets you set in *How To Target Your Actions On Success* (page 19)

- Carrying out, day in, day out, week in, week out, month in, month out, those actions, and *only* those actions, which contribute to your success. This means carrying out *all* the Four Must-Do Activities (page 5) in a *planned*, *regular* way

- Consistently **Staying On-Track**, seeking the simplest ways of doing things. The harder you make it for people to copy what you do, the fewer the people who can follow you

- Being a great supporter of meetings. As soon as you can, you should start your own sizzle sessions (page 22).

Teach your people the habit of Consistency!

BECOME A LEADER

Even if you want only a small group, you must lead from the front. There is no room for managers who sit at home telling other people to do what they do not do themselves. Accept responsibility for creating the success of your group, because no-one else is going to. Keep reminding yourself every day, throughout the day, that:

*The pace of the leader (that's **you**) dictates the pace of the pack.*

Your group looks to you. If you are not urgent, nor will they be. If you do not work hard, nor will they. If you do not do the right things, nor will they. And, if you falter, so will they. So every night ask yourself, *'If every one of my people did what I did today, how would my group grow?'*—and be honest with yourself! Did you really behave today like a person who leads from the front? Did you really give your people a good example?

Become an inspiration to your group—
and teach your people to do the same for theirs!

BUILD YOUR S.T.A.R. SUCCESS PYRAMID!

The ancient pyramids were built to last. By accident or design, every successful person, in whatever field, has built their success step by step with the same strong foundation.

All five levels are essential to the structure of the pyramid: the strength of each level is directly based on the strength of all the levels below. No matter how fit and strong the athlete, one tiny torn muscle can bring disaster and it is the same with your S.T.A.R. Success Pyramid: your business is only as strong as the weakest level, no matter how well the other levels have been constructed. Build each level as solidly as possible, because that is the only way to ensure that your Success Pyramid does not collapse into the rubble of failure.

The more each stage is reinforced, the greater your achievement will be.

The S.T.A.R. Success Pyramid gives you an easy to follow trouble-shooting chart. If your business is not succeeding as it should, you will be able to trace the problem to one or other of the five levels. Once you know the cause, you can seek the cure. In the same way, if you have a distributor whose business is not succeeding as it should, help them to evaluate the strength of each level in their Success Pyramid and they should be able to track down the problem.

YOUR ON-TRACK LANDMARKS

These landmarks will keep you On-Track. **The explanations are on the next page.** *To keep your people On-Track, take them through these landmarks!*

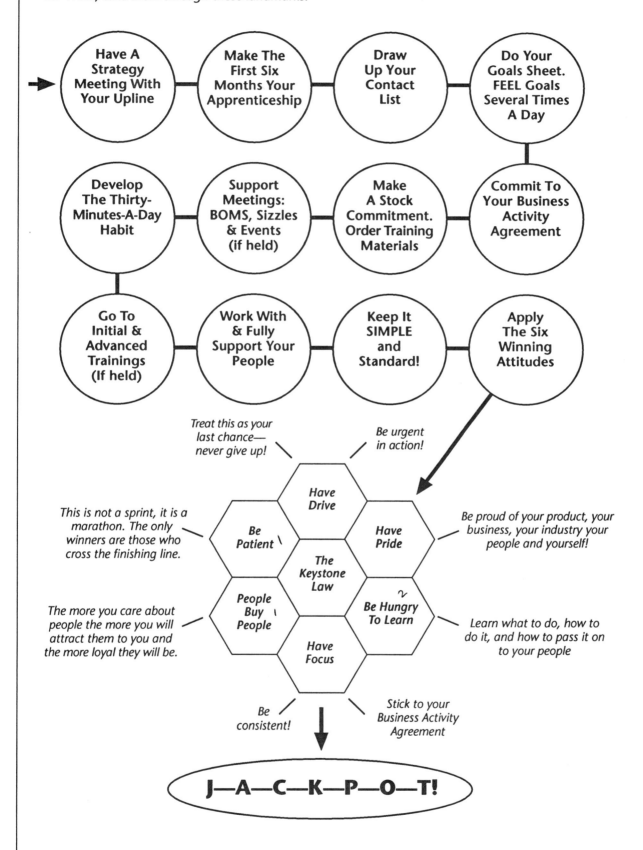

The Keystone Law: *Your path to success is ONLY through your people!*

WHAT DO YOUR ON-TRACK LANDMARKS MEAN?

(For more information on any of these terms, see the S.T.A.R. Leadership Programme)

A Strategy Meeting is held with an upline to plan the future of your business. If no experienced upline is available, I strongly recommend that you start the S.T.A.R. Leadership Programme (page 94) *now*. You have too much at stake not to.

The Six Months' Apprenticeship. Any new business needs to be learnt. Treat your first six months as your training period. If you are not going to listen, learn and apply what you have learnt with an open mind, is it worth your while to carry on?

The Contact List. Your list of *everyone* you know who has yet to join your business—you cannot succeed in network marketing without a comprehensive Contact List (see page 15 below).

Goals Sheet. The vivid, motivating summary of your goals which you review several times each day (see page 9 above).

The Business Activity Agreement. A distributor's agreement with themselves, committing them to take focused action to achieve their goals (see page 19 below).

Stock Commitment. You must be a user of the product and your own most devoted customer. You will sell a great deal more if you have samples to show.

The Importance of Meetings. This is part of the Business Activity Agreement (see above) but it is so important that it deserves a special mention.

The Thirty-Minutes-A-Day Habit is also part of the Business Activity Agreement. Devote 15 minutes a day to watching part of a video, listening to part of a tape, or reading a few pages of a book on network marketing, on your opportunity or on personal development. Then devote a further 15 minutes to reviewing a video, tape or book you've *already* studied (this helps you to stop complicating the business and Going Off-Track).

Go To Initial & Advanced Trainings (if held). This is a vital part of your Six Months' Apprenticeship. If your group does not hold them, go to any that are held by other groups—true network marketeers will always be happy to help crossline.

Working With. This is the best way to reduce drop-outs and generate momentum in your group. You must establish the habit of Working With throughout your business. *It is impossible to overemphasise the value of Working With*. Please refer to page 25 *NOW!*

Keep It Simple & Standard! The harder you make it for people to copy what you do, the fewer the people who can follow you. This also means, *don't try to reinvent the wheel!* Stick to the proven way of doing things.

Apply The Six Winning Attitudes. All six attitudes will speed the growth of your business. But above all, if you want anything more than a low-level business, success in network marketing needs *Drive* and *Focus*. This is such a once-in-a-lifetime opportunity for you to get what you want out of life that it is great shame to see the majority of distributors fail when just a little more determination would have got them there!

Don't you be one of those who looks back and thinks, 'If only…'. Be one of those who looks back and thinks, 'Thank heavens I never gave up, no matter how tempting it was at the time!'

To find out more about how to apply the Six Winning Attitudes, see my book *Get Off To A Winning Start In Network Marketing* (see page 93 for details).

Your Contact List

THE DOOR TO YOUR SUCCESS

Onto your Contact List (see page 32) should go everyone you can remember, going back as far as you can, no matter who they are, how long it is since you saw them or how little you know them. Your Contact List is the most important document in your possession: it is the foundation of your business. There is a saying among top distributors that if your house is on fire, forget everything else—*but get your Contact List out!*

Experienced network marketeers often refuse to work with a new distributor until they have done their Contact List because they have found out the hard way that no-one ever gets their business off the ground without it. That's how important it is.

Before you start your List, it is important to understand that you cannot tell beforehand who will or will not be interested and, if they do come into your business, who will or will not succeed. The most experienced distributors say that the *only* way they can tell who will succeed is by who is still with them after six months! Even if someone is not interested in the business, they might know someone who would be, or they may become a customer for the product, or they may know someone who would like to look at the products! There is just no way to tell in advance. And that person you rejected as being unsuitable—perhaps they know someone who would be a real star for you! So it is not who *you* know which matters, it is who *they* know.

So the rule is: *do not prejudge.* It is amazing how often distributors decide that someone they know would not be interested, perhaps because they think they are too busy or successful, only to find that someone else goes and signs them up!

If you do not show the product or the business to somebody, someone else will!

Get away from thinking that your job is to 'sell' the opportunity or the products to people, because it is not. 'Selling' to some people suggests putting pressure on people and there is no place for this in network marketing—you will only lose your friends and destroy the reputation of your business. Your job is only to sort the wheat from the chaff—those who are not interested from those who are. In other words, *you are in the sorting, not the sales, business.* So just *show* people—everyone you can find—the product and the opportunity and let them make up their own minds. And remember, *everyone* is a source of names for you.

You need to write down *everyone* you know because sponsoring is a question of timing; unless you are incredibly lucky, only a small number of the people you talk to will be interested in an opportunity at that particular moment. Don't worry about that because you only need a small number of people anyway. If you find only 5 active people and everyone else brings in only 5, by just 5 levels down you will have 781 active people in your business! But, to find that 5, you may need to talk to a lot of people. Let's say you start with only 10 people on your list, after selecting the contacts you judge will be the most interested. If the first 5 say 'No', you will be getting worried because, in your mind, half your contacts have let you down. But, if you have 100 names and you accept that you have no idea which of those 100 will be interested, you are not going to worry about 5 saying 'No'.

Finally, if *you* do not start your business with a proper Contact List, the people you bring in will not, either. They will follow your example. I can tell you now that, if that happens, you will *never* get your business off the ground.

THE FROGS SYSTEM FOR BUILDING YOUR CONTACT LIST

This is a pure numbers game. So you are going to have to kiss a lot of frogs to get your princes! The more people you see, the more you will sign. Do not be a sniper, picking off the odd target, be a machine gunner, firing at all and sundry.

Friends. Most people can easily remember the friends they see often. But check your address book and Christmas card list for those you see less frequently.

Relations. If you have few relatives, you will remember them easily. If your family is extended, again refer to your address book and Christmas card list, and ask close family members to check your list and add to it.

Organisations. The schools you attended (including the staff), the companies you have worked for (including the bosses and customers), the clubs and organisations you belong or have belonged to, all are sources of contacts.

Geographical:

1. Write down your neighbours where you live now

2. Note all your previous addresses, and write down all neighbours at each address at which you have lived

3. Think of everyone locally who is not a friend or relation, but whom you occasionally come across—your doctor, vicar, insurance broker, postman, milkman, accountant, solicitor, bank manager, receptionists, staff in shops, garages and so on. Do this for your previous addresses as well

4. Break the country into geographical areas and see if you can remember who you know in each area.

Social. This covers acquaintances who do not fit into any of the above categories. For instance, go through your list of friends again and try to remember who you met at their houses or at social occasions you attended with them. Do the same with your list of relatives and with neighbours you have visited.

CATEGORISING CONTACTS

You should categorise your contacts into two groups:

1. **Executive Contacts**: professionals, executives, managers, directors, salespeople, higher level entrepreneurs, businesspeople, and some people of a high social status or wealthy background

2. **Non-executive Contacts**: less high-powered entrepreneurs and businesspeople, and everyone else!

We said above, 'don't prejudge,' so why categorise? *Not* because people in one group may be more interested or more successful than people in the other. Your best contacts are those most determined and hungry for success, and they can come from either category. The *only* reason we categorise is because *some people need to be shown the business differently*:

- Executive contacts may be more influenced by how well the opportunity is presented to them or on the credibility of the person showing them than by the opportunity itself, and they are more likely to ask searching questions

- Non-executive Contacts may be less influenced by the way the business is presented, and are less likely to ask searching questions.

This means that you should only approach Executive Contacts either when you have developed some experience, or with the hands-on support of an experienced upline. Don't worry if it is not possible, but try to see *all* your contacts with an upline. Not only is this the best way to sponsor but it is the quickest way for you to learn. For the same reason, train your downlines only to see their contacts with an upline.

Finally, *keep your Contact List constantly updated.* Collect business cards wherever you are. Every time you meet someone new, add them to the list. No-one is ever removed from your List until you sponsor them. Even if they join another network, do not cross them off because it is quite common for people to try two or three networks before they find the one which leads to their success.

To work your Contact List, use a **Contact Box**. For this, you need:

- A set of large-sized filing cards, with filing box and a set of alphabet dividers

- A week-to-view diary, at least A5 (half the size of this page).

HOW TO PREPARE AND WORK YOUR CONTACT LIST

1. Make out your Contact List on pages 32 to 35. If you are working closely with your sponsor or an upline, have a photocopy ready for the Strategy Meeting (page 14). This is for their records, so that they can help you to work your List. Most experienced distributors will not work with you unless you give them a copy.

2. Find out which uplines will see contacts with you. Choose the best upline (called the **Compatible Upline**) for each contact and enter this upline's name in the right-hand column.

3. If a contact says 'Maybe' or 'No', cross their name off the Contact List and transfer their details to the card index system in the Contact Box, filed in alphabetic order.

4. Note on this card, the date of *every* approach you make to that contact (letter, phone or meeting), and the result.

5. Each time you get in touch, note in your diary the date on which you are next to get in touch. If they have become a retail customer, this of course is the next date you are to call about the product or reorders.

If you do a lot of retailing, you may want a second Contact Box just for your customers.

Timing is important. Very often, people do not join a network when they first look because, at that stage, there is nothing in it for them. Perhaps they are happy at work and are earning enough for their needs. But no jobs or businesses are secure today and it often happens that a few weeks, months or years later, they will badly need your opportunity. If you do not keep in regular touch during this period, you will lose them to someone who does happen to approach them at the right moment. *So it is important to follow up contacts frequently.* This is very simple: just phone every few months and ask, 'How are things going?' As soon as you have made the call, enter the contact's name into your diary for the next scheduled contact.

Used properly, this system matures. It will sponsor more people for you in years two and three than in year one—but not if you do not follow up properly!

Sponsoring Aids And Training Materials

KEEP TRACK OF YOUR LENDING

You will need suitable books, tapes and videos (**Sponsoring Aids**) to lend to prospective distributors. To help them evaluate your business, you can:

1. Send Sponsoring Aids out 'cold' with an accompanying letter (called a **Fishing Letter**) saying that you will follow up in a few days with a phone call, *or*

2. Lend them to a contact after you have phoned or met them.

You need two basic sets of sponsoring aids. Most Executive Contacts (see page 16) will prefer a low key, professional approach. Non-executive Contacts might prefer a more motivational sponsoring aid.

You will also need a stock of quality training materials, which are lent to new distributors to get them started pending delivery of their own materials. *Do not lend materials to distributors who are not prepared to order their own.* They are not taking their own business seriously, so why should you?

Sponsoring aids and training materials cost you money, so it is perfectly right and proper that they are lent, not given. If you are building your business properly, there could be a lot of these lent out at any one time, representing quite a substantial cash outlay to you, so it is important to get them back! This means that you need a recording system so that you can track who has what.

The lending procedure is as follows:

1. Put a numbered sticker on each item, for ease of identification. Also, some contacts will send them back with no covering note, and this is the only way you will know who they came from!

2. Put your name and address on each item. A pre-printed sticker looks much more professional and need not cost much

3. Enter each item against the relevant number on the Sponsoring Aids Location Form on page 36

4. When you lend any item, complete the recipient's details *in pencil* on the form. This is because, during its life, each item will be lent out to many people

5. If a contact has not returned an item after two weeks, chase up by phone or letter and enter the date on the Location Form. If by letter, enclose stamps for the return postage

6. Chase them just once more, two weeks after that. In my experience, if contacts do not return a sponsoring aid after being chased twice, they never will. However, distributors usually only need one reminder phone call

7. On the item's return, rub out the entry on the Sponsoring Aids Location Form. This tells you that this item is now available to be lent to someone else.

How To Target Your Actions On Success

OVERVIEW

This section is in two parts:

1. **A standardised individual work plan** for yourself and your downlines
2. **Group management plans** to help you manage your team as a whole.

1. SETTING AND USING INDIVIDUAL TARGETS

a. YOUR BUSINESS ACTIVITY AGREEMENT (OR 'BACTA')

> *Unless you know what you are supposed to achieve,*
> *how do you know you have achieved it?*

All business success is achieved by:

1. Knowing what you want to achieve
2. Setting targets to focus your actions on creating that achievement
3. Setting measurable standards to see how you are doing along the way.

Your Goals Sheet (page 9) covers point 1; your Business Activity Agreement (see page 37) deals with points 2 and 3.

The Business Activity Agreement covers the essential targets which every serious distributor will want to set themselves. It is an agreement you make with *yourself* (in other words, it is *not* what your uplines want of you) to achieve certain minimum targets under each of the Four Must-Do Activities (page 5) of Retailing, Sponsoring, Teaching and Attitudes. If you are receiving close help from an upline, it is also the level of activity you are prepared to put in, in return for their help.

My experience is that people who plan their work in this way achieve far more than those who do not because it keeps you *focused* on being a rocket—doing only those things which aim directly to your success—and helps you to avoid being a Catherine wheel, doing things which aim nowhere. Also,

> *If you write down that you will do something, you are more likely to do it.*

One of the great attractions of network marketing is that you are the boss. Unlike a job, where your employer tells you how much time you must put in, what your working hours are, and what they expect from you, in network marketing:

* *You* decide how much time you will give
* *You* decide what your working hours will be *and*
* *You* decide what you want from the business.

And, if an upline is working closely with you, *you* tell *them* what you want.

Having said that, how well you do will be a direct reflection of:

* The time you put in
* The working hours you choose, *and*
* How effectively you apply the Six Winning Attitudes during the time you give.

Although successful businesses can be built by people who can only manage week-ends, or evenings, or part-time day work, the more you limit yourself the longer it is going to take to reach your goals. Someone putting in 100 hours a week and prepared to work at any time required will clearly reach the level of business they want very much more quickly than someone who starts with 10 hours a week and is only prepared to work at certain times.

Once you decide what time you will devote to your new business and what you want to get from it, are your aims realistic? To take an exaggerated example, if you want to earn £5,000 a month within six months on ten hours work a week, this is unrealistic. Based on other people's experience in your network, find out what is realistic after six months on ten hours a week and, alternatively, how much work you must put in to reach earnings of £5,000 a month (I can tell you the answer to that for any network—seven days a week, with as many hours as you can find, over whatever period the history of your network shows is needed—although you can, of course, build up to that time input).

So this exercise gives you the information you need to decide: will you stick to ten hours a week and settle for a lower rate of growth, will you put in the all-out effort required to earn £5,000 a month as quickly as possible, or will you decide on something in-between? May I remind you that, whatever decision you make, it is *yours*. No-one can make you do anything you don't want to do.

But it is not just the time you are prepared to give which is important. Much more important are:

- What you do in that time, *and*
- The attitudes you bring to what you do.

In other words, the **quality** of your work also matters.

- Someone spending long hours on being a Catherine wheel will achieve far less than someone spending a few hours being a rocket
- Some people take far less time than others to do the same things, because the attitude they bring to what they do is better.

The targets you set yourself under your Business Activity Agreement will vary as your own circumstances or the needs of your business change. For instance:

- You may start part-time with the intention of going full-time as your business develops; your targets will gradually increase in line with this, *or*
- You may find that your targets were over-ambitious when you started; in this case, you will reduce them
- You could be a parent with more time available during term-time and less time in the holidays; your targets will vary accordingly
- You may be a professional using your network marketing business as an extra profit centre in addition to your core business; your targets could go up and down quite widely depending on how busy you are in your mainstream business, *or*
- You may be aiming to build a big business but need to earn quick money when you first sign up. You are facing a dilemma as the immediate money comes from retailing whereas the longer-term big money comes from sponsoring and business building. So at first you will need to set a high Retailing Target at the expense of sponsoring. But, as you begin to earn royalties from your downlines and the immediate pressure of income decreases, you should turn your attention to business building. To do this, you

would gradually reduce your Retailing Target while increasing the number of people you contact with a view to sponsoring by raising your Contacting Target.

The important things about your Business Activity Agreement are:

- That it is realistic in relation to the results you want to achieve

- That you feel comfortable with it—set it too high and you just won't bother to keep up with it, *and*

- That it is flexible and kept up-to-date in line with changing circumstances.

Make the Business Activity Agreement part of your habit of Consistency because, once you stop using it properly and keeping it up-to-date, you will become a Catherine wheel, not a rocket. *Working hard* is not the same as *Working smart*! Therefore, get into the habit of *consciously* recording every change to your Business Activity Agreement and *formally* advising any upline who is working closely with you. For this reason, use a pencil to complete your Business Activity Agreement, so that you can change it as often as you like, or make plenty of photocopies of the form for future use.

You will find your copy of the BACTA form on page 37. Here is what the targets mean…

The Retailing Target. This is the sales volume you aim to achieve. It may be a weekly or monthly target. If a target is monthly, there is a tendency to leave it until near the end of the month before 'going for it'; so, if the target can be divided into weekly chunks, it should be.

If you do not need to earn money immediately, perhaps because you have an income from another job, your spouse is working, or you have savings, *this does not mean that you do not have to set yourself a Retailing Target*. As people only earn from what is sold, there is not much point in having distributors who are not committed to selling anything. You would be amazed at how many big businesses there are in which no-one is earning very much because there is no commitment to retail sales! But, if there is no pressure for immediate income, your Retailing Target need not be high. Network marketing is a numbers game and it is remarkable how little each distributor needs to sell in order to earn you a big income, provided that you have enough distributors and everyone is selling *something*. Ask an upline what you would earn if you had 1,000 distributors averaging just one order a week—or even one a month, for that matter! So what would 5,000 distributors earn you?

You can express the Retailing Target in terms of number of orders, units of product sold, or cash value. If there is a figure you just *have* to earn from your business, including personal sales needed to qualify under your plan, cash value is probably best. But if you are in the fortunate position of not having to sell to survive, number of orders may suit you better.

The Contacting Targets. Your Personal Target means people contacted off your own Contact List and Contact Box. Your Downline Target means people contacted off your downlines' Contact Lists when Working With your downlines. You should begin to set yourself a Downline Target as soon as you have sponsored your first distributor.

People sometimes get confused about contacting targets. They do not mean how many people you sponsor, they mean how many people you *contact* with the aim of showing them the business. ***It does not matter whether they come into the business or not.*** In fact, every contact you make counts for your target *even if they refuse to have a look at the business.*

Unless you are very part-time, these should be set as a *daily* targets: contacting 25 people a week sounds much harder than 5 people a day from Monday to Friday. If you simply cannot make daily phone calls, spread the target over the days you *will* work. Specify which days those are and write them in the 'Notes' section on your BACTA. However, if you are very part-time, these can be set as weekly targets because the number you will contact each week is low anyway.

The Learning Target. This is your commitment to the Thirty-Minutes-A-Day Habit outlined on page 14. You will find it helpful to set aside a specific time each day for this activity. Immediately before you start your working day is safest.

The Meetings Targets. There is no doubt that regular attendance at meetings will help your business to grow. However, meetings can become a substitute for action, so don't overdo it. Your BACTA will help you to keep the balance right.

The BOM Target. If your company or group hold Business Opportunity Meetings, it is vital that you support them. If you do not, why should anyone else? Set yourself the goal of taking a guest to every BOM you attend.

The Sizzle Targets. A sizzle is a regular meeting of distributors for training and mutual support. If your upline holds a sizzle, write in the time on your Upline Sizzle Target and commit yourself to attending regularly.

To begin with, your Personal Sizzle Target will be 'nil' because as yet you have no-one in your business. Once you have sponsored two people, you should start your own sizzles. Although these are *your* sizzles, if possible invite uplines to chair and run them for you, until you have enough confidence and experience to run them on your own. If no experienced upline is available, my book *How To Lead A Winning Group* will show you how to run one.

Start your sizzles weekly on the same evening each week. This is important, first, because you and your top distributors need to be able to plan weeks ahead and, second, because your top distributors will eventually be holding their own sizzles and these obviously must be held on a different evening to yours.

Once your group gets too big, limit your sizzles to your top performing distributors (who may not always be your frontliners). As your group becomes established, you should find that the need for your personal sizzles drops to fortnightly and then monthly.

At first, your Downline Sizzle Target will also be 'nil'. Then, as each downline starts their own sizzle, you should run it for them until they are experienced enough to take over. Also, support your experienced downlines by sometimes appearing as a guest at their sizzles. These are the two activities covered by your Downline Sizzle Target.

The Two-to-One Target. This does not just refer to Two-to-Ones with your own contacts but also includes the Two-to-Ones you do with your downlines. Two-to-Ones are the absolute core of the business and the more you do the better. It does not matter who sponsors a new distributor—it is still another person coming into your business on whom you may earn royalty. Two-to-Ones are also a very important arena for training. The more you support your downlines by doing Two-to-Ones with them, the faster *your* business will grow!

Please note that when you are just starting out the Two-to-One Target does not apply because the number of Two-to-Ones you book will depend on the reaction to your phone calls, which is outside your control.

During your first weeks and over periods when your business is expanding fast, you may well be updating your Business Activity Agreement each week.

So once again, please remember to complete the form in pencil, or photocopy plenty of copies before you use it.

b. NEW DISTRIBUTOR BUSINESS ACTIVITY AGREEMENTS

There are six forms on page 38 for you to keep a record of the BACTAs of the new distributors with whom you are working closely. Complete these forms in pencil because you will need to change them constantly in line with a new distributor's evolving needs, or photocopy plenty copies of the blank form for future use. The new distributors should of course have their own copy of the Agreement, using the main BACTA form shown on page 37.

Although you should work closely with only a very few new distributors at a time (even six may be too many unless circumstances are exceptional), over the course of a year you should work with very many more. As each new person becomes trained, you will leave them and move on to Working With another new distributor. This means that the downlines with whom you are working closely will change constantly. (The new distributors you work with directly may have been sponsored either by you or by one of your downlines.)

If a downline wants you to help them build their business, you should make a Business Activity Agreement a condition of that help. Explain the following:

1. If they keep to their side of the bargain they can expect *your* full support in return

2. If they do not keep to their side of the agreement, you will stop Working With them. You will soon find that there is no mileage in trying to motivate people who will not help themselves. If that happens, either find another distributor who will welcome your help, or sponsor a new one. Apply the maxim *'It is easier to give birth than it is to raise the dead'* and you won't go far wrong

3. The Business Activity Agreement is *not* what you want of them, but what they feel comfortable with for themselves (this is not a business where it pays to try to get people to do more than they want)

4. They can change their Business Activity Agreement as often as they like but it is important that they do it properly by writing down their new targets and informing you as their upline—otherwise it will lose its disciplining and focusing effect on their business. Indeed, because it should reflect the changing needs of the business, the Business Activity Agreement is not being applied properly if it is *not* changed often!

5. The Two-to-One Target includes Two-to-Ones they do for downlines.

You should check how they actually spend their time against what their Business Activity Agreement says they should be doing at regular intervals (initially, on a daily basis), and make sure that they develop the same habit with *their* people.

Remember to record whether a distributor's BACTA targets are daily, weekly or monthly.

Remember, too, that the Two-to-One Target, the Downline Contacting Target and Downline Sizzle Target do not apply to new distributors in the very early stages of their business.

2. YOUR GROUP MANAGEMENT PLANS

Now you have the tools you need for individual planning, we will look at how you should plan and control the development of your group as a whole. Begin to use these leadership tools as soon as you have leaders starting to emerge and you feel you have the confidence. They only take a few minutes to complete each month, and will repay your effort many times over. To make the most of these tools, you will find it helpful to read my book *How To Lead A Winning Group*.

The tools you will need are:

- The **Business Progress Chart** (page 39), which keeps a running monthly summary of the performance of your group as a whole

- The **Top Leaders' Achievement Forms** (page 45), so that you know how much your leaders are planning to contribute to your overall group target

- **Monthly Action Plan** (page 40), which sets out in broad outline what you have to do to achieve your targets for the month

- **Monthly Activity Summary** (page 44), which summarises all the activities in your diary and shows in detail how you are spending your time to achieve your targets.

To use these tools, here is what you do:

1. Set out what you want your group to achieve for the coming month in the Business Progress Chart on page 39. At month end, enter what you actually achieved to see how well you did against target. Depending on your aims for the business, your main focus might be group turnover, numbers of new distributors, or numbers of distributors achieving promotion within the Compensation Plan. Different business goals and different Compensation Plans require different approaches, so ask experienced and successful uplines for guidance

2. Set up a monthly planning meeting (which may or may not coincide with a sizzle session), to discuss with your top people what their targets will be for the following month. Setting targets together helps to generate confidence, excitement and group momentum (as well as making sure that people keep the planning habit going!)

3. Now use your Monthly Action Plan on page 40 to answer the question: *What will I need to do to hit target this month?* At the planning meeting, total up the targets of your top leaders (if any of your leaders are downline of another leader in the planning group, be careful not to double-count their contributions). If there is a gap between what you want to achieve and your leaders' combined targets, how will you fill it? Should you start a new leg? Do some extra personal retailing? Set up a sponsoring or retailing incentive scheme? Or perhaps specific leaders will agree to raise their targets if you offer to work intensively in their group over the month to help them grow their businesses. For instance, you might suggest that if you were to help x number of people to promote themselves from position 'a' to position 'b', their group volume will automatically achieve your target. Then you could work out with your top leaders who you should offer to work with to get them promoted and hit the target. If you look like exceeding your group target, you have the luxury of making your own choice about where to focus your energies for the month—but you should still write down your strategic priorities both to keep the planning habit and to avoid losing focus.

4. If your network requires you to qualify each month for royalties (not all do), plan how you will achieve the necessary personal turnover and qualifications to avoid

missing out. If there is no qualification requirement, you must still set yourself a retailing target on your Business Activity Agreement. Plan how you will achieve that.

5. Finally, using your Monthly Action Plan to guide you, fill up as much of your Monthly Activity Summary (page 44) as you can. Book up the people you will be Working With as soon as possible, before they book something else. Aim to plan out and diary as much of each month as possible by the end of the previous month.

Not only should you use this system from Day 1 for yourself, but you should immediately start each new distributor on it as well, and make sure that they train their downlines to do the same.

THE SECRET OF GETTING PLANS TO WORK—'WORKING WITH'

If you can establish the planning habit within your group, you will have achieved a quantum leap in your prospects for success. But to re-emphasize one of the main themes of this book, planning alone is not enough. You have to help your people put their plans into action, and that means rolling up your sleeves and **Working With** them.

'Working With' means actually making contact phone calls with your people, actually going to see their contacts and customers with them, actually planning their work with them and actually going along to help them run their sizzle sessions. Make no mistake, this is much harder work than just telling people what to do, but *more than anything else*, people who create Working With as the training culture of their group predispose themselves and their people to success, but those who do not, predispose themselves and their people to failure.

- The more people work together, the less likely they are to drop out
- The more people work together, the more each will do.
- The more people work together, the quicker they will learn.
- The more people work together, the quicker their groups will build.

At this stage, you and your people will not be experienced and you may be worried that you are not good enough to go out and Work With them to show them what to do. Don't worry—two people working badly together will achieve much more—at least *five times* more—than each trying to work on their own! As well as the obvious advantages of each giving the other motivation and moral support, two people will learn very much more quickly together and will put in more action together than they would on their own.

Of course, the ideal is to get experienced uplines to Work With you and your people, but this is not always possible. Don't worry if you cannot get good upline help—although it is harder to build a business on your own, plenty of people have reached the top in this way! It just takes longer, that's all. You fill find all the help you need in the three books of my S.T.A.R. Leadership Programme.

If you have no upline help, it will pay you to find a **Co-Learner**. This is another new distributor, like yourself. Working together, you will each help the other over that vital early stage until you both have distributors in your own groups to Work With.

Your diary should never show you working on your own. Every entry should be Working With—upline, downline or crossline. If you want to do the best you can by your people, you should ban people from working on their own—it is soul-destroying, demotivating *and a major reason for drop-outs.*

So now you know how to plan, and how to get your plans to work. Put this knowledge into action and you will give yourself a huge head start over most people trying to make their way in this business.

Business Needs
& Recording Profits And Expenses

WHAT DO YOU NEED TO SET UP IN BUSINESS?

If you are already self-employed, much of this will already be familiar to you.

Car. Make sure your insurance covers you for business use. Check this covers samples (i.e., stock not for sale) and, if relevant, deliveries and stock for sale. If you do not have a car, building a business will be much more difficult but is not impossible, although it takes creativity with public transport or 'cadging' lifts.

Phone. However, it is impossible to do this job without a phone, and you should be prepared for a high phone bill. If you have not got a phone, reach agreement with someone else, not only to use theirs whenever you need it but for them to take a lot of messages for you when you are not there. Many old age pensioners or non-working single parents would be happy for the company and the chance to do something active in return for the use of their phone. But be fair—at least pay their *whole* bill, including the rental.

Answering machine. If you don't already have one, get one as soon as you can afford it. Nowadays you can pick up a basic machine very cheaply. Also, BT and other service providers offer answering services.

Your Sponsoring Aids and Training Materials Library. If you are serious about the business, this is an *essential* initial business expense and the more you can afford to buy and lend out, the quicker your business will build. One way to reduce the cost of these resources is to buy in bulk and supply your downlines. You win two ways. First, you are giving them convenient access to the best materials for learning and sponsoring, so they are more likely to use them. And, second, you will be making a retail profit, or you can pass on the discounts to your people—the choice is yours. But be sure to check with your uplines that you are not cutting across existing company or group arrangements.

Fax, mobile phone, computer, business cards and stationery, separate office. It is common to see new distributors lashing out on all sorts of unnecessary electronic gizmos and fancy cards and stationery but neglecting what they really need—their essential sponsoring aids and training materials library. Bearing in mind that they will not build your business more quickly, none of these bits and pieces are necessary. If you have spare cash available by all means get them, but I know top distributors earning five figures a month who have none of these things!

Leaflets. Cold market leafleting and mailshots are generally a waste of money unless you know what you are doing or have hands-on support from a successful upline. But, if you insist on doing it without upline support (and if your company allows it), do it properly! Tatty photocopies on low grade paper hardly give the image you are trying to portray of a potentially serious businessperson offering a high-level business opportunity!

You may well find that your company or uplines can sell you suitable materials. If not, you will have to produce your own. If you cannot afford single colour printing onto *quality* paper (probably a lot less expensive than you think, so get some quotes), you can save money, but still give the appearance of quality, by using tinted paper and/or a single colour print other than black. But watch the tints: some can look dull or dowdy. Your third option is **high quality** photocopying using 100 gsm paper (the copying shop will know what you mean).

You may sponsor low-calibre people, but what **serious** person will be attracted to your business by cheap leaflets? It rarely pays so, if you cannot afford quality, I strongly recommend that you save your money and concentrate on your warm market.

Bank accounts. If you are self-employed, a separate bank account is not essential because your personal and business affairs are not separated for income tax purposes. However, you might find it more convenient to open a separate personal account to be used purely for business and then transfer money from that to your private account as you need it. If you do this, do **not** call it a business account otherwise you may find that petrol stations, hotels, restaurants and so on refuse to accept cheques drawn on it even with a cheque guarantee card. Instead, call it 'No. 1' or 'No. 2' account.

DSS. If you are registered as unemployed and are drawing benefit, **discuss your position with your local office before you sign up with a network**. The rules on self-employment change frequently, but many DSS offices are very sympathetic to the fact that you may need to continue to draw benefit until income starts to come in from your business and will do all they can to help. It may also help to emphasise that this is a part-time business with flexible hours and that you are still available for work. If you have any difficulty, you may find that your local small business advice service can help you to negotiate with your DSS office.

If you do not advise the DSS of your new business and continue to draw benefit, **you will leave yourself open to legal action** even though you may not yet be drawing an income.

INCOME TAX

This is a complex area for self-employed people and full of pitfalls. Unless your business is very small indeed, you will find that it pays to take on an accountant. If you keep your records up-to-date yourself, and use your accountant only for occasional advice and for completing your tax returns, you may well find that is costs less than you think. A good accountant will often pay for themselves by pointing out claims and allowances which you would have missed.

At present, the Inland Revenue is heavily promoting the Self Assessment scheme. I advise you not to take that route: if you get things wrong the Revenue will hold you responsible and mistakes can prove expensive. For peace of mind, the modest cost of an accountant is well worthwhile.

To find a good accountant, ask your uplines and self-employed friends who they would recommend. Your bank manager and local small business advice service should also be able to help. You may find that your company or group run an accounting scheme: see how it compares with what you can find yourself.

When you approach an accountant, outline the service you require and ask for an estimated annual cost. For self-employed people, the best accountants are often self-employed themselves, working from home with low overheads.

Here are some of the key issues with income tax...

PAYE. If your network marketing business is not a limited company, and you currently pay income tax under a PAYE system (in other words, if you are currently employed), your network marketing earnings and expenses for tax purposes will be dealt with completely separately by the Inland Revenue. Again, my advice is to use an accountant.

Car, phone, home office. The rules here are complex and change frequently. If you do not have an accountant, ask your Tax Inspector for advice.

Hotels, entertainment. Contrary to what many people think, you may not be able to offset against tax the cost of booking rooms for meetings or interviews, or buying refreshments for people in your business. This whole area is messy, because there are, equally, occasions on which you *can* claim! Ignorance is no excuse where tax is concerned so make sure you understand the rules.

Export. If you have customers or distributors overseas, you will need to take advice. For example, you may be able to offset against tax any expenses associated with foreign businesspeople coming to the UK to see you, even though you cannot reclaim on the same expenses associated with home-based businesspeople.

SHOULD YOU BE VAT REGISTERED?

Some companies require you to register for VAT when you reach a certain level on the compensation plan. The idea fills many people with dread but there is no real need to worry. Registration is quick and painless: contact your local Customs and Excise and they will send you all the information you need plus a form which is easy to fill in. Although being registered will require a little more book keeping, it is not as bad as people make out provided you keep your books in good order.

If you are already VAT registered as a sole trader you have no choice—you must include your network marketing business in that registration. However, if you are a director of a limited company which is VAT registered but intend to run your network marketing business as a sole trader, the VAT status of the limited company is not relevant: you can register or not as you choose.

However, once your business turns over more than a certain figure in any 12 month period (£47,000 at the time of writing), you are required by law to be VAT registered, therefore a good accountant's advice is essential to ensure that you stay within the law. If your turnover is under the compulsory registration limit, registration is optional but there may nevertheless be advantages in becoming registered, as you can reclaim VAT on all your outlays. Once again, the answer is to get competent professional advice.

Where VAT is concerned, be very careful about 'going it alone'. It is almost impossible for the lay person understand all the ins and outs of the regulations, and mistakes can be costly. If you have any questions about VAT, your local VAT Enquiry service gives helpful free advice. To find them, look under Customs and Excise in your local phone book.

THE IMPORTANCE OF RECORDING INCOME AND EXPENDITURE

Most expenses of running a business can be set against tax. This could save you around 25p in every £1. In other words, if you don't claim back everything you can, you could be throwing away a quarter of all your income from the business! Most people find keeping accounts an absolute bore—but it will feel much more worthwhile if you remember the savings you are making!

There is another powerful argument for keeping proper books. Although your outlays in a network marketing business will be relatively low compared to other forms of business, they can still add up. If you do not keep track of your expenses, you will have no real idea of how much money your business is making.

If you don't keep on top of your expenses, they will get on top of you! Once you fall behind, not only is it a terrible job to get your records straight but, inevitably, you will never remember everything you could have claimed. So get into the habit of recording your expenses daily on the Monthly Expenditure Record (page 69). It takes no time at all to do this and, if you make it a regular habit, your books will never become a problem.

HOW TO COMPLETE THE MONTHLY FINANCIAL RECORDS

Please read these instructions carefully, and re-read them from time to time until you are thoroughly familiar with the system.

SETTING UP YOUR SYSTEM

The system in this book should meet all your needs during your first year of trading. It is also a very simple way of accounting for VAT. However if you prefer, you can use an A4-sized analysis book, or an inexpensive computer software package (but be sure it has the potential to handle VAT as you may well need this feature in the future). Computerised accounts have the advantage of doing all the calculations for you and eliminating the possibility of arithmetical mistakes but, unless you are a good typist, data entry can be slower. If you choose to set up your own system, base your headings on the ones I give in the monthly records on pages 68 and 69. Accountants charge by the amount of work they have to do, so make sure that your bookkeeping method is convenient for them: most accountants are more than happy if you use the system in this book.

Set aside a regular time each day (or at worst, each week) to keep your accounts up-to -date.

RECEIPTS & INVOICES

- As a filing system, you will need an inexpensive ring binder. Use monthly dividers and set up separate sections for your receipts and invoices. File everything in date order so your accountant can find it easily. You may find it convenient to file your bank statements and credit card statements in the same binder. Keep all records (originals, *not* copies) for at least six years in case Inland Revenue or VAT require you to produce them.

- Get invoices or receipts for everything you can. A receipt is proof to the tax inspector that you incurred that expense.

- If you cannot get a receipt (parking meters, small incidental expenses, etc.), record the date, amount and nature of the expense in a handy notebook as soon as possible, before you forget it. Next time you do your accounts, write out a petty cash voucher for each outlay and file it with your other receipts (you can use pre-printed pads, but a note on a plain sheet of paper is fine). A lot of people don't bother with this but small amounts soon add up. Remember, each sum claimed could be worth 25p in the £1 to you.

- Note on each receipt the column (page 69) under which it is entered in your accounts.

- Issue an invoice for every sale and keep a copy for your records. If your company cannot supply you, you can find pre-printed pads at any business stationer.

BANK STATEMENTS & CREDIT CARD STATEMENTS

- Get your bank to send a monthly statement which goes from the 1st of each month, then cross-check it against your Monthly Record. Also, check your monthly credit card statements against the Monthly Record.

- From the monthly statements, enter all standing orders, bank and credit card charges etc. into the Monthly Record, otherwise you will be worse off than you think.

MAKING PAYMENTS AND PAY-INS

- Payments by cheque: record the date, amount and who you are paying on the cheque stub. Then enter the date and cheque number on the relevant invoice or receipt.

- Payments by credit card: always ask for a separate receipt because credit card vouchers are not accepted by the Inland Revenue or VAT.

- Bank pay-ins: using your pay-in book, record the date of each pay-in together with the cash sums, and the names, numbers and amounts of each cheque.

WORKING WITH THE MONTHLY INCOME RECORD (page 68)

- **IMPORTANT!** If you are not VAT registered, record the *full* amount of all your income in columns B,C and D. Ignore columns E and F (you can cross them out if you like). Then enter the amount again in the Gross Income column (I will show you later how to use this column to check your addition).

- **IMPORTANT!** If you are VAT registered, you need to separate out the VAT content of your income for the VAT Inspector. This can be done quite easily. For every transaction where you have charged VAT, enter the amount *excluding the VAT content* in column B, C or D as appropriate. Then, on the same row, enter the amount of VAT involved in column E (VAT Content). If the invoice has no VAT content, enter the whole amount in column F (Misc. Non-Vatable Income). Finally, for both vatable and non-vatable income, enter the total amount (the total of columns B to F) in column G (Gross Income).

- Whenever you make a payment into the bank, record it on a new row on your Monthly Income Record. Enter the date, the description 'Bank pay-in' in column A, and record the amount in column H (Total Banked).

- At month end, cross-check the total of column G (Gross Income) against the combined total of columns B, C, and D (plus E and F if you are using them). If the two totals are not identical, you have made an error. I stress this because most people don't bother to do this and this often involves them in a lot of extra fees caused by the accountant having to check every balance for the whole year to find where the errors are.

WORKING WITH THE MONTHLY EXPENDITURE RECORD (page 69)

- In column I (Method) enter the method of payment. Note the last three figures of the cheque number for a cheque payment, or 'D/D' for a payment by Direct Debit, 'S/O' for a payment by Standing Order, and 'Csh' for a cash payment.

- Record *all* business expenses. Whether or not they are allowable for tax purposes, they are still a cost of running your business and have therefore reduced your profit. To take an exaggerated example, let's say that your profit for the month was £1,000. You might be quite pleased with that. But, what if non-allowable outlays on meetings and entertainment had cost you £500 and you had not recorded that on your accounts? Although your 'book' profit is £1,000, your actual 'take home' profit is now only £500—and it is your actual 'take home' profit which really interests you. Your accountant will go through your accounts and make an adjustment for non-claimable items before completing your tax return.

- **IMPORTANT!** If you are not VAT registered, do not use columns O (VAT Content) and Q (Misc Non-Vatable Expenditure). Simply enter the full amount involved in the appropriate column, and repeat the figure in column R (Gross Expenditure). If you are

VAT registered, proceed as before, entering vatable expenditure in columns J to N *excluding their VAT content*, and the VAT content into column O. Use column Q for non-vatable expenditure. Then enter the total sum for the transaction in the Gross Expenditure column. At month end, check that the combined totals of columns J to Q are equal to the total of column R (Gross Expenditure).

- The Cumulative Running Total column (column S) is provided to enable you to keep track of the balance of your bank account or any other balance you choose. This can be particularly useful if money is tight. When you set up your books, simply use the current balance as a starting point, then add every incoming payment and subtract every expenditure as you go along.

KEEPING TRACK OF YOUR PROFITS

The final form in the book is titled Cumulative Profit/Loss For The Year (page 92). This will show you the financial results of all your efforts: your profit or loss for the year to date, as well as your profit or loss for the month.

At the end of every month, transfer the totals from your Monthly Record onto this summary form, writing the name of the month in the space in the left hand column. The difference between your income and expenditure is your profit or loss. Add each figure to the total in the 'Year to date' row above to give you the running total to date.

If you are VAT registered, you can also use the Cumulative Profit/Loss For The Year form to automatically give you the figures you need for your quarterly VAT return. You will find additional instructions in the Notes on the form itself. Please note that you may also have to make an extra VAT payment for the use of your car: the rules are complex and you will need to take professional advice.

Finally, *make sure you submit your VAT returns and payments on time*. Inspectors move as soon as you become overdue and the penalties are very harsh!

Contact List

No.	Name & Town	Occupation	Age	Phone	Category 1	Category 2	Upline Chosen For 2-to-1
1							
2							
3							
4							
5							
6							
7							
8							
9							
10							
11							
12							
13							
14							
15							
16							
17							
18							
19							
20							
21							
22							
23							
24							
25							
26							
27							
28							
29							
30							
31							
32							
33							
34							
35							
36							
37							
38							
39							
40							
41							
42							
43							
44							
45							
46							
47							
48							
49							
50							

Contact List *(continued...)*

No.	Name & Town	Occupation	Age	Phone	Category 1	2	Upline Chosen For 2-to-1
51							
52							
53							
54							
55							
56							
57							
58							
59							
60							
61							
62							
63							
64							
65							
66							
67							
68							
69							
70							
71							
72							
73							
74							
75							
76							
77							
78							
79							
80							
81							
82							
83							
84							
85							
86							
87							
88							
89							
90							
91							
92							
93							
94							
95							
96							
97							
98							
99							
100							

Contact List (continued...)

No.	Name & Town	Occupation	Age	Phone	Category 1	Category 2	Upline Chosen For 2-to-1
101							
102							
103							
104							
105							
106							
107							
108							
109							
110							
111							
112							
113							
114							
115							
116							
117							
118							
119							
120							
121							
122							
123							
124							
125							
126							
127							
128							
129							
130							
131							
132							
133							
134							
135							
136							
137							
138							
139							
140							
141							
142							
143							
144							
145							
146							
147							
148							
149							
150							

Contact List (continued...)

No.	Name & Town	Occupation	Age	Phone	Category 1	Category 2	Upline Chosen For 2-to-1
151							
152							
153							
154							
155							
156							
157							
158							
159							
160							
161							
162							
163							
164							
165							
166							
167							
168							
169							
170							
171							
172							
173							
174							
175							
176							
177							
178							
179							
180							
181							
182							
183							
184							
185							
186							
187							
188							
189							
190							
191							
192							
193							
194							
195							
196							
197							
198							
199							
200							

Sponsoring Aids Location Form (complete in pencil)

No.	Sponsoring Aid	Tape Video Book	Lent to...	Date	Date 1st Chase	Date 2nd Chase
1						
2						
3						
4						
5						
6						
7						
8						
9						
10						
11						
12						
13						
14						
15						
16						
17						
18						
19						
20						
21						
22						
23						
24						
25						
26						
27						
28						
29						
30						
31						
32						
33						
34						
35						
36						
37						
38						
39						
40						
41						
42						
43						
44						
45						
46						
47						
48						
49						
50						

Business Activity Agreement (complete in pencil)

General targets:

My Retailing Target is:		per week/per month
My Personal Contacting Target is:		per day/per week
My Downline Contacting Target is:		per day/per week
My Learning Target:	For my Thirty-Minutes-A-Day Habit I will set aside for study the time from _____ o'clock to _____ o'clock each day	

Meeting targets:

BOM Target*	I accept that I must attend **at least** one BOM every week. My weekly BOM target is _____	
Upline Sizzle*	I accept that I must attend **every** session of my upline's sizzle, currently held each week/fortnight/month on _____ at _____ o'clock	
Personal Sizzle†	I will hold my own sizzle, each week/fortnight/month on _____ at _____ o'clock	
My Downline Sizzle Target is:		per week
My Two-to-One Target is:		per week

Notes:

Sponsor + Retail + Teach + Attitudes + Sponsor + Retail + Teach + Attitudes

* These targets are only relevant if the meetings exist in your company or group
† You should start your personal sizzle as soon as you have recruited two people

New Distributor BACTA Summary

Name: *Updated:* / /

General Targets:

Retailing Target	
Personal Contacting Target	
Downline Contacting Target	

Meeting Targets:

BOM Target	
Upline Sizzle Target	
Personal Sizzle Target	
Downline Sizzle Target	
Two-to-One Target	

Name: *Updated:* / /

General Targets:

Retailing Target	
Personal Contacting Target	
Downline Contacting Target	

Meeting Targets:

BOM Target	
Upline Sizzle Target	
Personal Sizzle Target	
Downline Sizzle Target	
Two-to-One Target	

Name: *Updated:* / /

General Targets:

Retailing Target	
Personal Contacting Target	
Downline Contacting Target	

Meeting Targets:

BOM Target	
Upline Sizzle Target	
Personal Sizzle Target	
Downline Sizzle Target	
Two-to-One Target	

Name: *Updated:* / /

General Targets:

Retailing Target	
Personal Contacting Target	
Downline Contacting Target	

Meeting Targets:

BOM Target	
Upline Sizzle Target	
Personal Sizzle Target	
Downline Sizzle Target	
Two-to-One Target	

Name: *Updated:* / /

General Targets:

Retailing Target	
Personal Contacting Target	
Downline Contacting Target	

Meeting Targets:

BOM Target	
Upline Sizzle Target	
Personal Sizzle Target	
Downline Sizzle Target	
Two-to-One Target	

Name: *Updated:* / /

General Targets:

Retailing Target	
Personal Contacting Target	
Downline Contacting Target	

Meeting Targets:

BOM Target	
Upline Sizzle Target	
Personal Sizzle Target	
Downline Sizzle Target	
Two-to-One Target	

Business Progress Chart

Month												
Target Group Turnover £££s												
Actual Group Turnover £££s												
Distributors at start of month												
New distributors												
Distributors at end of month												

Number of Distributors at each position on the compensation plan
(Enter titles in the numbered boxes below)

1.												
2.												
3.												
4.												
5.												
6.												
7.												
9.												
10.												
11.												
12.												

Notes:

Action Plan For The Month Of _____

What must I do to qualify?

What must I do to hit my group target?

Action Plan For The Month Of _____

What must I do to qualify?

What must I do to hit my group target?

Action Plan For The Month Of _____

What must I do to qualify?

What must I do to hit my group target?

Action Plan For The Month Of _____

What must I do to qualify?
What must I do to hit my group target?

Action Plan For The Month Of _____

What must I do to qualify?
What must I do to hit my group target?

Action Plan For The Month Of _____

What must I do to qualify?
What must I do to hit my group target?

Action Plan For The Month Of _____

What must I do to qualify?

What must I do to hit my group target?

Action Plan For The Month Of _____

What must I do to qualify?

What must I do to hit my group target?

Action Plan For The Month Of _____

What must I do to qualify?

What must I do to hit my group target?

Action Plan For The Month Of _____

What must I do to qualify?

What must I do to hit my group target?

_____
_____
_____
_____
_____
_____
_____
_____
_____
_____
_____
_____
_____

Action Plan For The Month Of _____

What must I do to qualify?

What must I do to hit my group target?

_____
_____
_____
_____
_____
_____
_____
_____
_____
_____
_____
_____
_____

Action Plan For The Month Of _____

What must I do to qualify?

What must I do to hit my group target?

_____
_____
_____
_____
_____
_____
_____
_____
_____
_____

Monthly Activity Summary

for the month of _____ *199___*

Date	Strategy Meetings	Retailing Visits	Contacting Calls	Two-to-Ones	BOMs/Sizzles/ Trainings
1					
2					
3					
4					
5					
6					
7					
8					
9					
10					
11					
12					
13					
14					
15					
16					
17					
18					
19					
20					
21					
22					
23					
24					
25					
26					
27					
28					
29					
30					
31					

Name:

Level: Position:

Total Distributors In Group	
Aiming for Promotion this Month?	Yes / No

Group Targets:	Target	Achieved
Group Volume £		
New Distributors In Group		
Number Promoted in Group		

Business Activity Agreement:	Target	Achieved
Personal Retailing		
Personal Contacting		
Downline Contacting		
Attending Two-to-Ones		
Attending BOMs		
Attending Downline Sizzles		

Name:

Level: Position:

Total Distributors In Group	
Aiming for Promotion this Month?	Yes / No

Group Targets:	Target	Achieved
Group Volume £		
New Distributors In Group		
Number Promoted in Group		

Business Activity Agreement:	Target	Achieved
Personal Retailing		
Personal Contacting		
Downline Contacting		
Attending Two-to-Ones		
Attending BOMs		
Attending Downline Sizzles		

Name:

Level: Position:

Total Distributors In Group	
Aiming for Promotion this Month?	Yes / No

Group Targets:	Target	Achieved
Group Volume £		
New Distributors In Group		
Number Promoted in Group		

Business Activity Agreement:	Target	Achieved
Personal Retailing		
Personal Contacting		
Downline Contacting		
Attending Two-to-Ones		
Attending BOMs		
Attending Downline Sizzles		

Name:

Level: Position:

Total Distributors In Group	
Aiming for Promotion this Month?	Yes / No

Group Targets:	Target	Achieved
Group Volume £		
New Distributors In Group		
Number Promoted in Group		

Business Activity Agreement:	Target	Achieved
Personal Retailing		
Personal Contacting		
Downline Contacting		
Attending Two-to-Ones		
Attending BOMs		
Attending Downline Sizzles		

Name:

Level: Position:

Total Distributors In Group	
Aiming for Promotion this Month?	Yes / No

Group Targets:	Target	Achieved
Group Volume £		
New Distributors In Group		
Number Promoted in Group		

Business Activity Agreement:	Target	Achieved
Personal Retailing		
Personal Contacting		
Downline Contacting		
Attending Two-to-Ones		
Attending BOMs		
Attending Downline Sizzles		

Name:

Level: Position:

Total Distributors In Group	
Aiming for Promotion this Month?	Yes / No

Group Targets:	Target	Achieved
Group Volume £		
New Distributors In Group		
Number Promoted in Group		

Business Activity Agreement:	Target	Achieved
Personal Retailing		
Personal Contacting		
Downline Contacting		
Attending Two-to-Ones		
Attending BOMs		
Attending Downline Sizzles		

Monthly Activity Summary

for the month of _____ *199*____

Date	Strategy Meetings	Retailing Visits	Contacting Calls	Two-to-Ones	BOMs/Sizzles/ Trainings
1					
2					
3					
4					
5					
6					
7					
8					
9					
10					
11					
12					
13					
14					
15					
16					
17					
18					
19					
20					
21					
22					
23					
24					
25					
26					
27					
28					
29					
30					
31					

Name:

Level:	Position:		
Total Distributors In Group			
Aiming for Promotion this Month?		Yes / No	

Group Targets:	Target	Achieved
Group Volume £		
New Distributors In Group		
Number Promoted in Group		

Business Activity Agreement:	Target	Achieved
Personal Retailing		
Personal Contacting		
Downline Contacting		
Attending Two-to-Ones		
Attending BOMs		
Attending Downline Sizzles		

Name:

Level:	Position:		
Total Distributors In Group			
Aiming for Promotion this Month?		Yes / No	

Group Targets:	Target	Achieved
Group Volume £		
New Distributors In Group		
Number Promoted in Group		

Business Activity Agreement:	Target	Achieved
Personal Retailing		
Personal Contacting		
Downline Contacting		
Attending Two-to-Ones		
Attending BOMs		
Attending Downline Sizzles		

Name:

Level:	Position:		
Total Distributors In Group			
Aiming for Promotion this Month?		Yes / No	

Group Targets:	Target	Achieved
Group Volume £		
New Distributors In Group		
Number Promoted in Group		

Business Activity Agreement:	Target	Achieved
Personal Retailing		
Personal Contacting		
Downline Contacting		
Attending Two-to-Ones		
Attending BOMs		
Attending Downline Sizzles		

Name:

Level:	Position:		
Total Distributors In Group			
Aiming for Promotion this Month?		Yes / No	

Group Targets:	Target	Achieved
Group Volume £		
New Distributors In Group		
Number Promoted in Group		

Business Activity Agreement:	Target	Achieved
Personal Retailing		
Personal Contacting		
Downline Contacting		
Attending Two-to-Ones		
Attending BOMs		
Attending Downline Sizzles		

Name:

Level:	Position:		
Total Distributors In Group			
Aiming for Promotion this Month?		Yes / No	

Group Targets:	Target	Achieved
Group Volume £		
New Distributors In Group		
Number Promoted in Group		

Business Activity Agreement:	Target	Achieved
Personal Retailing		
Personal Contacting		
Downline Contacting		
Attending Two-to-Ones		
Attending BOMs		
Attending Downline Sizzles		

Name:

Level:	Position:		
Total Distributors In Group			
Aiming for Promotion this Month?		Yes / No	

Group Targets:	Target	Achieved
Group Volume £		
New Distributors In Group		
Number Promoted in Group		

Business Activity Agreement:	Target	Achieved
Personal Retailing		
Personal Contacting		
Downline Contacting		
Attending Two-to-Ones		
Attending BOMs		
Attending Downline Sizzles		

Monthly Activity Summary   *for the month of* _____ 199____

Date	Strategy Meetings	Retailing Visits	Contacting Calls	Two-to-Ones	BOMs/Sizzles/ Trainings
1					
2					
3					
4					
5					
6					
7					
8					
9					
10					
11					
12					
13					
14					
15					
16					
17					
18					
19					
20					
21					
22					
23					
24					
25					
26					
27					
28					
29					
30					
31					

Name:

Level: Position:

Total Distributors In Group	
Aiming for Promotion this Month?	Yes / No

Group Targets:	Target	Achieved
Group Volume £		
New Distributors In Group		
Number Promoted in Group		

Business Activity Agreement:	Target	Achieved
Personal Retailing		
Personal Contacting		
Downline Contacting		
Attending Two-to-Ones		
Attending BOMs		
Attending Downline Sizzles		

Name:

Level: Position:

Total Distributors In Group	
Aiming for Promotion this Month?	Yes / No

Group Targets:	Target	Achieved
Group Volume £		
New Distributors In Group		
Number Promoted in Group		

Business Activity Agreement:	Target	Achieved
Personal Retailing		
Personal Contacting		
Downline Contacting		
Attending Two-to-Ones		
Attending BOMs		
Attending Downline Sizzles		

Name:

Level: Position:

Total Distributors In Group	
Aiming for Promotion this Month?	Yes / No

Group Targets:	Target	Achieved
Group Volume £		
New Distributors In Group		
Number Promoted in Group		

Business Activity Agreement:	Target	Achieved
Personal Retailing		
Personal Contacting		
Downline Contacting		
Attending Two-to-Ones		
Attending BOMs		
Attending Downline Sizzles		

Name:

Level: Position:

Total Distributors In Group	
Aiming for Promotion this Month?	Yes / No

Group Targets:	Target	Achieved
Group Volume £		
New Distributors In Group		
Number Promoted in Group		

Business Activity Agreement:	Target	Achieved
Personal Retailing		
Personal Contacting		
Downline Contacting		
Attending Two-to-Ones		
Attending BOMs		
Attending Downline Sizzles		

Name:

Level: Position:

Total Distributors In Group	
Aiming for Promotion this Month?	Yes / No

Group Targets:	Target	Achieved
Group Volume £		
New Distributors In Group		
Number Promoted in Group		

Business Activity Agreement:	Target	Achieved
Personal Retailing		
Personal Contacting		
Downline Contacting		
Attending Two-to-Ones		
Attending BOMs		
Attending Downline Sizzles		

Name:

Level: Position:

Total Distributors In Group	
Aiming for Promotion this Month?	Yes / No

Group Targets:	Target	Achieved
Group Volume £		
New Distributors In Group		
Number Promoted in Group		

Business Activity Agreement:	Target	Achieved
Personal Retailing		
Personal Contacting		
Downline Contacting		
Attending Two-to-Ones		
Attending BOMs		
Attending Downline Sizzles		

Monthly Activity Summary

for the month of _____ **199**____

Date	Strategy Meetings	Retailing Visits	Contacting Calls	Two-to-Ones	BOMs/Sizzles/ Trainings
1					
2					
3					
4					
5					
6					
7					
8					
9					
10					
11					
12					
13					
14					
15					
16					
17					
18					
19					
20					
21					
22					
23					
24					
25					
26					
27					
28					
29					
30					
31					

Name:

Level: Position:

Total Distributors In Group		
Aiming for Promotion this Month?		Yes / No

Group Targets:	Target	Achieved
Group Volume £		
New Distributors In Group		
Number Promoted in Group		

Business Activity Agreement:	Target	Achieved
Personal Retailing		
Personal Contacting		
Downline Contacting		
Attending Two-to-Ones		
Attending BOMs		
Attending Downline Sizzles		

Name:

Level: Position:

Total Distributors In Group		
Aiming for Promotion this Month?		Yes / No

Group Targets:	Target	Achieved
Group Volume £		
New Distributors In Group		
Number Promoted in Group		

Business Activity Agreement:	Target	Achieved
Personal Retailing		
Personal Contacting		
Downline Contacting		
Attending Two-to-Ones		
Attending BOMs		
Attending Downline Sizzles		

Name:

Level: Position:

Total Distributors In Group		
Aiming for Promotion this Month?		Yes / No

Group Targets:	Target	Achieved
Group Volume £		
New Distributors In Group		
Number Promoted in Group		

Business Activity Agreement:	Target	Achieved
Personal Retailing		
Personal Contacting		
Downline Contacting		
Attending Two-to-Ones		
Attending BOMs		
Attending Downline Sizzles		

Name:

Level: Position:

Total Distributors In Group		
Aiming for Promotion this Month?		Yes / No

Group Targets:	Target	Achieved
Group Volume £		
New Distributors In Group		
Number Promoted in Group		

Business Activity Agreement:	Target	Achieved
Personal Retailing		
Personal Contacting		
Downline Contacting		
Attending Two-to-Ones		
Attending BOMs		
Attending Downline Sizzles		

Name:

Level: Position:

Total Distributors In Group		
Aiming for Promotion this Month?		Yes / No

Group Targets:	Target	Achieved
Group Volume £		
New Distributors In Group		
Number Promoted in Group		

Business Activity Agreement:	Target	Achieved
Personal Retailing		
Personal Contacting		
Downline Contacting		
Attending Two-to-Ones		
Attending BOMs		
Attending Downline Sizzles		

Name:

Level: Position:

Total Distributors In Group		
Aiming for Promotion this Month?		Yes / No

Group Targets:	Target	Achieved
Group Volume £		
New Distributors In Group		
Number Promoted in Group		

Business Activity Agreement:	Target	Achieved
Personal Retailing		
Personal Contacting		
Downline Contacting		
Attending Two-to-Ones		
Attending BOMs		
Attending Downline Sizzles		

Monthly Activity Summary

for the month of _____ **199___**

Date	Strategy Meetings	Retailing Visits	Contacting Calls	Two-to-Ones	BOMs/Sizzles/ Trainings
1					
2					
3					
4					
5					
6					
7					
8					
9					
10					
11					
12					
13					
14					
15					
16					
17					
18					
19					
20					
21					
22					
23					
24					
25					
26					
27					
28					
29					
30					
31					

Top Leaders Achievement Forms

for the month of _____ **199___**

Name:

Level: Position:

Total Distributors In Group	
Aiming for Promotion this Month?	Yes / No

Group Targets:	Target	Achieved
Group Volume £		
New Distributors In Group		
Number Promoted in Group		

Business Activity Agreement:	Target	Achieved
Personal Retailing		
Personal Contacting		
Downline Contacting		
Attending Two-to-Ones		
Attending BOMs		
Attending Downline Sizzles		

Name:

Level: Position:

Total Distributors In Group	
Aiming for Promotion this Month?	Yes / No

Group Targets:	Target	Achieved
Group Volume £		
New Distributors In Group		
Number Promoted in Group		

Business Activity Agreement:	Target	Achieved
Personal Retailing		
Personal Contacting		
Downline Contacting		
Attending Two-to-Ones		
Attending BOMs		
Attending Downline Sizzles		

Name:

Level: Position:

Total Distributors In Group	
Aiming for Promotion this Month?	Yes / No

Group Targets:	Target	Achieved
Group Volume £		
New Distributors In Group		
Number Promoted in Group		

Business Activity Agreement:	Target	Achieved
Personal Retailing		
Personal Contacting		
Downline Contacting		
Attending Two-to-Ones		
Attending BOMs		
Attending Downline Sizzles		

Name:

Level: Position:

Total Distributors In Group	
Aiming for Promotion this Month?	Yes / No

Group Targets:	Target	Achieved
Group Volume £		
New Distributors In Group		
Number Promoted in Group		

Business Activity Agreement:	Target	Achieved
Personal Retailing		
Personal Contacting		
Downline Contacting		
Attending Two-to-Ones		
Attending BOMs		
Attending Downline Sizzles		

Name:

Level: Position:

Total Distributors In Group	
Aiming for Promotion this Month?	Yes / No

Group Targets:	Target	Achieved
Group Volume £		
New Distributors In Group		
Number Promoted in Group		

Business Activity Agreement:	Target	Achieved
Personal Retailing		
Personal Contacting		
Downline Contacting		
Attending Two-to-Ones		
Attending BOMs		
Attending Downline Sizzles		

Name:

Level: Position:

Total Distributors In Group	
Aiming for Promotion this Month?	Yes / No

Group Targets:	Target	Achieved
Group Volume £		
New Distributors In Group		
Number Promoted in Group		

Business Activity Agreement:	Target	Achieved
Personal Retailing		
Personal Contacting		
Downline Contacting		
Attending Two-to-Ones		
Attending BOMs		
Attending Downline Sizzles		

Monthly Activity Summary
for the month of _____ 199____

Date	Strategy Meetings	Retailing Visits	Contacting Calls	Two-to-Ones	BOMs/Sizzles/ Trainings
1					
2					
3					
4					
5					
6					
7					
8					
9					
10					
11					
12					
13					
14					
15					
16					
17					
18					
19					
20					
21					
22					
23					
24					
25					
26					
27					
28					
29					
30					
31					

Name:

Level: Position:

Total Distributors In Group	
Aiming for Promotion this Month?	Yes / No

Group Targets:	Target	Achieved
Group Volume £		
New Distributors In Group		
Number Promoted in Group		

Business Activity Agreement:	Target	Achieved
Personal Retailing		
Personal Contacting		
Downline Contacting		
Attending Two-to-Ones		
Attending BOMs		
Attending Downline Sizzles		

Name:

Level: Position:

Total Distributors In Group	
Aiming for Promotion this Month?	Yes / No

Group Targets:	Target	Achieved
Group Volume £		
New Distributors In Group		
Number Promoted in Group		

Business Activity Agreement:	Target	Achieved
Personal Retailing		
Personal Contacting		
Downline Contacting		
Attending Two-to-Ones		
Attending BOMs		
Attending Downline Sizzles		

Name:

Level: Position:

Total Distributors In Group	
Aiming for Promotion this Month?	Yes / No

Group Targets:	Target	Achieved
Group Volume £		
New Distributors In Group		
Number Promoted in Group		

Business Activity Agreement:	Target	Achieved
Personal Retailing		
Personal Contacting		
Downline Contacting		
Attending Two-to-Ones		
Attending BOMs		
Attending Downline Sizzles		

Name:

Level: Position:

Total Distributors In Group	
Aiming for Promotion this Month?	Yes / No

Group Targets:	Target	Achieved
Group Volume £		
New Distributors In Group		
Number Promoted in Group		

Business Activity Agreement:	Target	Achieved
Personal Retailing		
Personal Contacting		
Downline Contacting		
Attending Two-to-Ones		
Attending BOMs		
Attending Downline Sizzles		

Name:

Level: Position:

Total Distributors In Group	
Aiming for Promotion this Month?	Yes / No

Group Targets:	Target	Achieved
Group Volume £		
New Distributors In Group		
Number Promoted in Group		

Business Activity Agreement:	Target	Achieved
Personal Retailing		
Personal Contacting		
Downline Contacting		
Attending Two-to-Ones		
Attending BOMs		
Attending Downline Sizzles		

Name:

Level: Position:

Total Distributors In Group	
Aiming for Promotion this Month?	Yes / No

Group Targets:	Target	Achieved
Group Volume £		
New Distributors In Group		
Number Promoted in Group		

Business Activity Agreement:	Target	Achieved
Personal Retailing		
Personal Contacting		
Downline Contacting		
Attending Two-to-Ones		
Attending BOMs		
Attending Downline Sizzles		

Monthly Activity Summary

for the month of _____ 199____

Date	Strategy Meetings	Retailing Visits	Contacting Calls	Two-to-Ones	BOMs/Sizzles/ Trainings
1					
2					
3					
4					
5					
6					
7					
8					
9					
10					
11					
12					
13					
14					
15					
16					
17					
18					
19					
20					
21					
22					
23					
24					
25					
26					
27					
28					
29					
30					
31					

Name:

Level: Position:

Total Distributors In Group		
Aiming for Promotion this Month?		Yes / No

Group Targets:	Target	Achieved
Group Volume £		
New Distributors In Group		
Number Promoted in Group		

Business Activity Agreement:	Target	Achieved
Personal Retailing		
Personal Contacting		
Downline Contacting		
Attending Two-to-Ones		
Attending BOMs		
Attending Downline Sizzles		

Name:

Level: Position:

Total Distributors In Group		
Aiming for Promotion this Month?		Yes / No

Group Targets:	Target	Achieved
Group Volume £		
New Distributors In Group		
Number Promoted in Group		

Business Activity Agreement:	Target	Achieved
Personal Retailing		
Personal Contacting		
Downline Contacting		
Attending Two-to-Ones		
Attending BOMs		
Attending Downline Sizzles		

Name:

Level: Position:

Total Distributors In Group		
Aiming for Promotion this Month?		Yes / No

Group Targets:	Target	Achieved
Group Volume £		
New Distributors In Group		
Number Promoted in Group		

Business Activity Agreement:	Target	Achieved
Personal Retailing		
Personal Contacting		
Downline Contacting		
Attending Two-to-Ones		
Attending BOMs		
Attending Downline Sizzles		

Name:

Level: Position:

Total Distributors In Group		
Aiming for Promotion this Month?		Yes / No

Group Targets:	Target	Achieved
Group Volume £		
New Distributors In Group		
Number Promoted in Group		

Business Activity Agreement:	Target	Achieved
Personal Retailing		
Personal Contacting		
Downline Contacting		
Attending Two-to-Ones		
Attending BOMs		
Attending Downline Sizzles		

Name:

Level: Position:

Total Distributors In Group		
Aiming for Promotion this Month?		Yes / No

Group Targets:	Target	Achieved
Group Volume £		
New Distributors In Group		
Number Promoted in Group		

Business Activity Agreement:	Target	Achieved
Personal Retailing		
Personal Contacting		
Downline Contacting		
Attending Two-to-Ones		
Attending BOMs		
Attending Downline Sizzles		

Name:

Level: Position:

Total Distributors In Group		
Aiming for Promotion this Month?		Yes / No

Group Targets:	Target	Achieved
Group Volume £		
New Distributors In Group		
Number Promoted in Group		

Business Activity Agreement:	Target	Achieved
Personal Retailing		
Personal Contacting		
Downline Contacting		
Attending Two-to-Ones		
Attending BOMs		
Attending Downline Sizzles		

Monthly Activity Summary

for the month of _____ 199___

Date	Strategy Meetings	Retailing Visits	Contacting Calls	Two-to-Ones	BOMs/Sizzles/ Trainings
1					
2					
3					
4					
5					
6					
7					
8					
9					
10					
11					
12					
13					
14					
15					
16					
17					
18					
19					
20					
21					
22					
23					
24					
25					
26					
27					
28					
29					
30					
31					

Top Leaders Achievement Forms

Name:

Level: Position:

Total Distributors In Group	
Aiming for Promotion this Month?	Yes / No

Group Targets:	Target	Achieved
Group Volume £		
New Distributors In Group		
Number Promoted in Group		

Business Activity Agreement:	Target	Achieved
Personal Retailing		
Personal Contacting		
Downline Contacting		
Attending Two-to-Ones		
Attending BOMs		
Attending Downline Sizzles		

Name:

Level: Position:

Total Distributors In Group	
Aiming for Promotion this Month?	Yes / No

Group Targets:	Target	Achieved
Group Volume £		
New Distributors In Group		
Number Promoted in Group		

Business Activity Agreement:	Target	Achieved
Personal Retailing		
Personal Contacting		
Downline Contacting		
Attending Two-to-Ones		
Attending BOMs		
Attending Downline Sizzles		

Name:

Level: Position:

Total Distributors In Group	
Aiming for Promotion this Month?	Yes / No

Group Targets:	Target	Achieved
Group Volume £		
New Distributors In Group		
Number Promoted in Group		

Business Activity Agreement:	Target	Achieved
Personal Retailing		
Personal Contacting		
Downline Contacting		
Attending Two-to-Ones		
Attending BOMs		
Attending Downline Sizzles		

Name:

Level: Position:

Total Distributors In Group	
Aiming for Promotion this Month?	Yes / No

Group Targets:	Target	Achieved
Group Volume £		
New Distributors In Group		
Number Promoted in Group		

Business Activity Agreement:	Target	Achieved
Personal Retailing		
Personal Contacting		
Downline Contacting		
Attending Two-to-Ones		
Attending BOMs		
Attending Downline Sizzles		

Name:

Level: Position:

Total Distributors In Group	
Aiming for Promotion this Month?	Yes / No

Group Targets:	Target	Achieved
Group Volume £		
New Distributors In Group		
Number Promoted in Group		

Business Activity Agreement:	Target	Achieved
Personal Retailing		
Personal Contacting		
Downline Contacting		
Attending Two-to-Ones		
Attending BOMs		
Attending Downline Sizzles		

Name:

Level: Position:

Total Distributors In Group	
Aiming for Promotion this Month?	Yes / No

Group Targets:	Target	Achieved
Group Volume £		
New Distributors In Group		
Number Promoted in Group		

Business Activity Agreement:	Target	Achieved
Personal Retailing		
Personal Contacting		
Downline Contacting		
Attending Two-to-Ones		
Attending BOMs		
Attending Downline Sizzles		

| Monthly Activity Summary | | | | for the month of _____ 199____ |
Date	Strategy Meetings	Retailing Visits	Contacting Calls	Two-to-Ones	BOMs/Sizzles/ Trainings
1					
2					
3					
4					
5					
6					
7					
8					
9					
10					
11					
12					
13					
14					
15					
16					
17					
18					
19					
20					
21					
22					
23					
24					
25					
26					
27					
28					
29					
30					
31					

Name:

Level: Position:

	Target	Achieved
Total Distributors In Group		
Aiming for Promotion this Month?	Yes / No	
Group Targets:	Target	Achieved
Group Volume £		
New Distributors In Group		
Number Promoted in Group		
Business Activity Agreement:	Target	Achieved
Personal Retailing		
Personal Contacting		
Downline Contacting		
Attending Two-to-Ones		
Attending BOMs		
Attending Downline Sizzles		

Name:

Level: Position:

	Target	Achieved
Total Distributors In Group		
Aiming for Promotion this Month?	Yes / No	
Group Targets:	Target	Achieved
Group Volume £		
New Distributors In Group		
Number Promoted in Group		
Business Activity Agreement:	Target	Achieved
Personal Retailing		
Personal Contacting		
Downline Contacting		
Attending Two-to-Ones		
Attending BOMs		
Attending Downline Sizzles		

Name:

Level: Position:

	Target	Achieved
Total Distributors In Group		
Aiming for Promotion this Month?	Yes / No	
Group Targets:	Target	Achieved
Group Volume £		
New Distributors In Group		
Number Promoted in Group		
Business Activity Agreement:	Target	Achieved
Personal Retailing		
Personal Contacting		
Downline Contacting		
Attending Two-to-Ones		
Attending BOMs		
Attending Downline Sizzles		

Name:

Level: Position:

	Target	Achieved
Total Distributors In Group		
Aiming for Promotion this Month?	Yes / No	
Group Targets:	Target	Achieved
Group Volume £		
New Distributors In Group		
Number Promoted in Group		
Business Activity Agreement:	Target	Achieved
Personal Retailing		
Personal Contacting		
Downline Contacting		
Attending Two-to-Ones		
Attending BOMs		
Attending Downline Sizzles		

Name:

Level: Position:

	Target	Achieved
Total Distributors In Group		
Aiming for Promotion this Month?	Yes / No	
Group Targets:	Target	Achieved
Group Volume £		
New Distributors In Group		
Number Promoted in Group		
Business Activity Agreement:	Target	Achieved
Personal Retailing		
Personal Contacting		
Downline Contacting		
Attending Two-to-Ones		
Attending BOMs		
Attending Downline Sizzles		

Name:

Level: Position:

	Target	Achieved
Total Distributors In Group		
Aiming for Promotion this Month?	Yes / No	
Group Targets:	Target	Achieved
Group Volume £		
New Distributors In Group		
Number Promoted in Group		
Business Activity Agreement:	Target	Achieved
Personal Retailing		
Personal Contacting		
Downline Contacting		
Attending Two-to-Ones		
Attending BOMs		
Attending Downline Sizzles		

Monthly Activity Summary

for the month of _____ 199___

Date	Strategy Meetings	Retailing Visits	Contacting Calls	Two-to-Ones	BOMs/Sizzles/ Trainings
1					
2					
3					
4					
5					
6					
7					
8					
9					
10					
11					
12					
13					
14					
15					
16					
17					
18					
19					
20					
21					
22					
23					
24					
25					
26					
27					
28					
29					
30					
31					
Date	Strategy Meetings	Retailing Visits	Contacting Calls	Two-to-Ones	BOMs/Sizzles/ Trainings

Name:

Level: Position:

	Target	Achieved
Total Distributors In Group		
Aiming for Promotion this Month?	Yes / No	
Group Targets:	Target	Achieved
Group Volume £		
New Distributors In Group		
Number Promoted in Group		
Business Activity Agreement:	Target	Achieved
Personal Retailing		
Personal Contacting		
Downline Contacting		
Attending Two-to-Ones		
Attending BOMs		
Attending Downline Sizzles		

Name:

Level: Position:

	Target	Achieved
Total Distributors In Group		
Aiming for Promotion this Month?	Yes / No	
Group Targets:	Target	Achieved
Group Volume £		
New Distributors In Group		
Number Promoted in Group		
Business Activity Agreement:	Target	Achieved
Personal Retailing		
Personal Contacting		
Downline Contacting		
Attending Two-to-Ones		
Attending BOMs		
Attending Downline Sizzles		

Name:

Level: Position:

	Target	Achieved
Total Distributors In Group		
Aiming for Promotion this Month?	Yes / No	
Group Targets:	Target	Achieved
Group Volume £		
New Distributors In Group		
Number Promoted in Group		
Business Activity Agreement:	Target	Achieved
Personal Retailing		
Personal Contacting		
Downline Contacting		
Attending Two-to-Ones		
Attending BOMs		
Attending Downline Sizzles		

Name:

Level: Position:

	Target	Achieved
Total Distributors In Group		
Aiming for Promotion this Month?	Yes / No	
Group Targets:	Target	Achieved
Group Volume £		
New Distributors In Group		
Number Promoted in Group		
Business Activity Agreement:	Target	Achieved
Personal Retailing		
Personal Contacting		
Downline Contacting		
Attending Two-to-Ones		
Attending BOMs		
Attending Downline Sizzles		

Name:

Level: Position:

	Target	Achieved
Total Distributors In Group		
Aiming for Promotion this Month?	Yes / No	
Group Targets:	Target	Achieved
Group Volume £		
New Distributors In Group		
Number Promoted in Group		
Business Activity Agreement:	Target	Achieved
Personal Retailing		
Personal Contacting		
Downline Contacting		
Attending Two-to-Ones		
Attending BOMs		
Attending Downline Sizzles		

Name:

Level: Position:

	Target	Achieved
Total Distributors In Group		
Aiming for Promotion this Month?	Yes / No	
Group Targets:	Target	Achieved
Group Volume £		
New Distributors In Group		
Number Promoted in Group		
Business Activity Agreement:	Target	Achieved
Personal Retailing		
Personal Contacting		
Downline Contacting		
Attending Two-to-Ones		
Attending BOMs		
Attending Downline Sizzles		

Monthly Activity Summary   *for the month of* _____ *199*____

Date	Strategy Meetings	Retailing Visits	Contacting Calls	Two-to-Ones	BOMs/Sizzles/ Trainings
1					
2					
3					
4					
5					
6					
7					
8					
9					
10					
11					
12					
13					
14					
15					
16					
17					
18					
19					
20					
21					
22					
23					
24					
25					
26					
27					
28					
29					
30					
31					

Top Leaders Achievement Forms

for the month of _____ 199____

Name:

Level: Position:

	Target	Achieved
Total Distributors In Group		
Aiming for Promotion this Month?	Yes / No	

Group Targets:	Target	Achieved
Group Volume £		
New Distributors In Group		
Number Promoted in Group		

Business Activity Agreement:	Target	Achieved
Personal Retailing		
Personal Contacting		
Downline Contacting		
Attending Two-to-Ones		
Attending BOMs		
Attending Downline Sizzles		

Name:

Level: Position:

	Target	Achieved
Total Distributors In Group		
Aiming for Promotion this Month?	Yes / No	

Group Targets:	Target	Achieved
Group Volume £		
New Distributors In Group		
Number Promoted in Group		

Business Activity Agreement:	Target	Achieved
Personal Retailing		
Personal Contacting		
Downline Contacting		
Attending Two-to-Ones		
Attending BOMs		
Attending Downline Sizzles		

Name:

Level: Position:

	Target	Achieved
Total Distributors In Group		
Aiming for Promotion this Month?	Yes / No	

Group Targets:	Target	Achieved
Group Volume £		
New Distributors In Group		
Number Promoted in Group		

Business Activity Agreement:	Target	Achieved
Personal Retailing		
Personal Contacting		
Downline Contacting		
Attending Two-to-Ones		
Attending BOMs		
Attending Downline Sizzles		

Name:

Level: Position:

	Target	Achieved
Total Distributors In Group		
Aiming for Promotion this Month?	Yes / No	

Group Targets:	Target	Achieved
Group Volume £		
New Distributors In Group		
Number Promoted in Group		

Business Activity Agreement:	Target	Achieved
Personal Retailing		
Personal Contacting		
Downline Contacting		
Attending Two-to-Ones		
Attending BOMs		
Attending Downline Sizzles		

Name:

Level: Position:

	Target	Achieved
Total Distributors In Group		
Aiming for Promotion this Month?	Yes / No	

Group Targets:	Target	Achieved
Group Volume £		
New Distributors In Group		
Number Promoted in Group		

Business Activity Agreement:	Target	Achieved
Personal Retailing		
Personal Contacting		
Downline Contacting		
Attending Two-to-Ones		
Attending BOMs		
Attending Downline Sizzles		

Name:

Level: Position:

	Target	Achieved
Total Distributors In Group		
Aiming for Promotion this Month?	Yes / No	

Group Targets:	Target	Achieved
Group Volume £		
New Distributors In Group		
Number Promoted in Group		

Business Activity Agreement:	Target	Achieved
Personal Retailing		
Personal Contacting		
Downline Contacting		
Attending Two-to-Ones		
Attending BOMs		
Attending Downline Sizzles		

Monthly Activity Summary

for the month of _____ 199____

Date	Strategy Meetings	Retailing Visits	Contacting Calls	Two-to-Ones	BOMs/Sizzles/ Trainings
1					
2					
3					
4					
5					
6					
7					
8					
9					
10					
11					
12					
13					
14					
15					
16					
17					
18					
19					
20					
21					
22					
23					
24					
25					
26					
27					
28					
29					
30					
31					

Name:

Level: Position:

Total Distributors In Group	
Aiming for Promotion this Month?	Yes / No

Group Targets:	Target	Achieved
Group Volume £		
New Distributors In Group		
Number Promoted in Group		

Business Activity Agreement:	Target	Achieved
Personal Retailing		
Personal Contacting		
Downline Contacting		
Attending Two-to-Ones		
Attending BOMs		
Attending Downline Sizzles		

Name:

Level: Position:

Total Distributors In Group	
Aiming for Promotion this Month?	Yes / No

Group Targets:	Target	Achieved
Group Volume £		
New Distributors In Group		
Number Promoted in Group		

Business Activity Agreement:	Target	Achieved
Personal Retailing		
Personal Contacting		
Downline Contacting		
Attending Two-to-Ones		
Attending BOMs		
Attending Downline Sizzles		

Name:

Level: Position:

Total Distributors In Group	
Aiming for Promotion this Month?	Yes / No

Group Targets:	Target	Achieved
Group Volume £		
New Distributors In Group		
Number Promoted in Group		

Business Activity Agreement:	Target	Achieved
Personal Retailing		
Personal Contacting		
Downline Contacting		
Attending Two-to-Ones		
Attending BOMs		
Attending Downline Sizzles		

Name:

Level: Position:

Total Distributors In Group	
Aiming for Promotion this Month?	Yes / No

Group Targets:	Target	Achieved
Group Volume £		
New Distributors In Group		
Number Promoted in Group		

Business Activity Agreement:	Target	Achieved
Personal Retailing		
Personal Contacting		
Downline Contacting		
Attending Two-to-Ones		
Attending BOMs		
Attending Downline Sizzles		

Name:

Level: Position:

Total Distributors In Group	
Aiming for Promotion this Month?	Yes / No

Group Targets:	Target	Achieved
Group Volume £		
New Distributors In Group		
Number Promoted in Group		

Business Activity Agreement:	Target	Achieved
Personal Retailing		
Personal Contacting		
Downline Contacting		
Attending Two-to-Ones		
Attending BOMs		
Attending Downline Sizzles		

Name:

Level: Position:

Total Distributors In Group	
Aiming for Promotion this Month?	Yes / No

Group Targets:	Target	Achieved
Group Volume £		
New Distributors In Group		
Number Promoted in Group		

Business Activity Agreement:	Target	Achieved
Personal Retailing		
Personal Contacting		
Downline Contacting		
Attending Two-to-Ones		
Attending BOMs		
Attending Downline Sizzles		

Monthly Income Record

for the month of _____ 199____

	A	B		C		D		E		F		G		H	
Date	Description	Bonuses & Product Sales		Trainings & Events		Misc. Income		VAT Content		Misc. Non-Vatable Income		Gross Income (Total: cols B-F)		Total Banked	
		£	p	£	p	£	p	£	p	£	p	£	p	£	p
1															
2															
3															
4															
5															
6															
7															
8															
9															
10															
11															
12															
13															
14															
15															
16															
17															
18															
19															
20															
21															
22															
23															
24															
25															
26															
27															
28															
29															
30															
31															
32															
33															
34															
35															
36															
37															
38															
39															
40															
41															
42															
43															
44															
45															
46															
47															
48															
49															
50															
	Monthly Totals														

Monthly Expenditure Record

I	J		K		L		M		N		O		P		Q		R		S	
Method Ch#, Csh D/D, S/O	Petrol, Oil & Vehicle Service		Hotel, Travel & Subsistence		Admin. & Phone		Product & Samples		Misc. Expenditure		VAT Content		Postage		Misc. Non-Vatable Expenditure		Gross Expenditure (Total: cols J-Q)		Cumulative Running Total	
	£	p	£	p	£	p	£	p	£	p	£	p	£	p	£	p	£	p	£	p
Totals																				

Monthly Income Record

for the month of _____ 199____

	A	B		C		D		E		F		G		H
Date	Description	Bonuses & Product Sales		Trainings & Events		Misc. Income		VAT Content		Misc. Non-Vatable Income		Gross Income (Total: cols B-F)		Total Banked
		£	p	£	p	£	p	£	p	£	p	£	p	£
1														
2														
3														
4														
5														
6														
7														
8														
9														
10														
11														
12														
13														
14														
15														
16														
17														
18														
19														
20														
21														
22														
23														
24														
25														
26														
27														
28														
29														
30														
31														
32														
33														
34														
35														
36														
37														
38														
39														
40														
41														
42														
43														
44														
45														
46														
47														
48														
49														
50														
	Monthly Totals													

Monthly Expenditure Record

I	J		K		L		M		N		O		P		Q		R		S	
Method Ch#, Csh D/D, S/O	Petrol, Oil & Vehicle Service		Hotel, Travel & Subsistence		Admin. & Phone		Product & Samples		Misc. Expenditure		VAT Content		Postage		Misc. Non- Vatable Expenditure		Gross Expenditure (Total: cols J-Q)		Cumulative Running Total	
	£	p	£	p	£	p	£	p	£	p	£	p	£	p	£	p	£	p	£	p
1																				
2																				
3																				
4																				
5																				
6																				
7																				
8																				
9																				
10																				
11																				
12																				
13																				
14																				
15																				
16																				
17																				
18																				
19																				
20																				
Totals																				

Monthly Income Record

for the month of _____ 199____

	Date	A Description	B Bonuses & Product Sales		C Trainings & Events		D Misc. Income		E VAT Content		F Misc. Non-Vatable Income		G Gross Income (Total: cols B-F)		H Total Banked	
			£	p	£	p	£	p	£	p	£	p	£	p	£	p
1																
2																
3																
4																
5																
6																
7																
8																
9																
10																
11																
12																
13																
14																
15																
16																
17																
18																
19																
20																
21																
22																
23																
24																
25																
26																
27																
28																
29																
30																
31																
32																
33																
34																
35																
36																
37																
38																
39																
40																
41																
42																
43																
44																
45																
46																
47																
48																
49																
50																
		Monthly Totals														

Monthly Expenditure Record

I	J		K		L		M		N		O		P		Q		R		S	
Method Ch#, Csh D/D, S/O	Petrol, Oil & Vehicle Service		Hotel, Travel & Subsistence		Admin. & Phone		Product & Samples		Misc. Expenditure		VAT Content		Postage		Misc. Non-Vatable Expenditure		Gross Expenditure (Total: cols J-Q)		Cumulative Running Total	
	£	p	£	p	£	p	£	p	£	p	£	p	£	p	£	p	£	p	£	p
1																				
2																				
3																				
4																				
5																				
6																				
7																				
8																				
9																				
10																				
11																				
12																				
13																				
14																				
15																				
16																				
17																				
18																				
Totals																				

Monthly Income Record

for the month of _____ 199___

	Date	A Description	B Bonuses & Product Sales £	p	C Trainings & Events £	p	D Misc. Income £	p	E VAT Content £	p	F Misc. Non-Vatable Income £	p	G Gross Income (Total: cols B-F) £	p	H Total Banked £	
1																
2																
3																
4																
5																
6																
7																
8																
9																
10																
11																
12																
13																
14																
15																
16																
17																
18																
19																
20																
21																
22																
23																
24																
25																
26																
27																
28																
29																
30																
31																
32																
33																
34																
35																
36																
37																
38																
39																
40																
41																
42																
43																
44																
45																
46																
47																
48																
49																
50																
		Monthly Totals														

Monthly Expenditure Record

I	J		K		L		M		N		O		P		Q		R		S	
Method Ch#, Csh D/D, S/O	Petrol, Oil & Vehicle Service		Hotel, Travel & Subsistence		Admin. & Phone		Product & Samples		Misc. Expenditure		VAT Content		Postage		Misc. Non-Vatable Expenditure		Gross Expenditure (Total: cols J-Q)		Cumulative Running Total	
	£	p	£	p	£	p	£	p	£	p	£	p	£	p	£	p	£	p	£	p
Totals																				

75

Monthly Income Record

for the month of _____ **199___**

	A	B		C		D		E		F		G		H	
Date	Description	Bonuses & Product Sales		Trainings & Events		Misc. Income		VAT Content		Misc. Non-Vatable Income		Gross Income (Total: cols B-F)		Total Banked	
		£	p	£	p	£	p	£	p	£	p	£	p	£	p
1															
2															
3															
4															
5															
6															
7															
8															
9															
10															
11															
12															
13															
14															
15															
16															
17															
18															
19															
20															
21															
22															
23															
24															
25															
26															
27															
28															
29															
30															
31															
32															
33															
34															
35															
36															
37															
38															
39															
40															
41															
42															
43															
44															
45															
46															
47															
48															
49															
50															
	Monthly Totals														

Monthly Expenditure Record

I	J		K		L		M		N		O		P		Q		R		S	
Method Ch#, Csh D/D, S/O	Petrol, Oil & Vehicle Service		Hotel, Travel & Subsistence		Admin. & Phone		Product & Samples		Misc. Expenditure		VAT Content		Postage		Misc. Non-Vatable Expenditure		Gross Expenditure (Total: cols J-Q)		Cumulative Running Total	
	£	p	£	p	£	p	£	p	£	p	£	p	£	p	£	p	£	p	£	p
Totals																				

Monthly Income Record

for the month of _____ 199___

		A	B Bonuses & Product Sales		C Trainings & Events		D Misc. Income		E VAT Content		F Misc. Non-Vatable Income		G Gross Income (Total: cols B-F)		H Total Banked	
	Date	Description	£	p	£	p	£	p	£	p	£	p	£	p	£	
1																
2																
3																
4																
5																
6																
7																
8																
9																
10																
11																
12																
13																
14																
15																
16																
17																
18																
19																
20																
21																
22																
23																
24																
25																
26																
27																
28																
29																
30																
31																
32																
33																
34																
35																
36																
37																
38																
39																
40																
41																
42																
43																
44																
45																
46																
47																
48																
49																
50																
		Monthly Totals														

Monthly Expenditure Record

	I	J		K		L		M		N		O		P		Q		R		S	
	Method Ch#, Csh D/D, S/O	Petrol, Oil & Vehicle Service		Hotel, Travel & Subsistence		Admin. & Phone		Product & Samples		Misc. Expenditure		VAT Content		Postage		Misc. Non- Vatable Expenditure		Gross Expenditure (Total: cols J-Q)		Cumulative Running Total	
		£	p	£	p	£	p	£	p	£	p	£	p	£	p	£	p	£	p	£	p
1																					
2																					
3																					
4																					
5																					
6																					
7																					
8																					
9																					
10																					
11																					
12																					
13																					
14																					
15																					
16																					
17																					
18																					
19																					
20																					
21																					
22																					
23																					
24																					
25																					
26																					
27																					
28																					
29																					
30																					
31																					
32																					
33																					
34																					
35																					
36																					
37																					
38																					
39																					
40																					
41																					
42																					
43																					
44																					
45																					
46																					
47																					
48																					
49																					
50																					
Totals																					

Monthly Income Record

for the month of _____ 199____

	A	B		C		D		E		F		G		H	
Date	Description	Bonuses & Product Sales		Trainings & Events		Misc. Income		VAT Content		Misc. Non-Vatable Income		Gross Income (Total: cols B-F)		Total Banked	
		£	p	£	p	£	p	£	p	£	p	£	p	£	p
1															
2															
3															
4															
5															
6															
7															
8															
9															
10															
11															
12															
13															
14															
15															
16															
17															
18															
19															
20															
21															
22															
23															
24															
25															
26															
27															
28															
29															
30															
31															
32															
33															
34															
35															
36															
37															
38															
39															
40															
41															
42															
43															
44															
45															
46															
47															
48															
49															
50															
	Monthly Totals														

Monthly Expenditure Record

I	J	K	L	M	N	O	P	Q	R	S
Method Ch#, Csh D/D, S/O	Petrol, Oil & Vehicle Service	Hotel, Travel & Subsistence	Admin. & Phone	Product & Samples	Misc. Expenditure	VAT Content	Postage	Misc. Non-Vatable Expenditure	Gross Expenditure (Total: cols J-Q)	Cumulative Running Total
	£ p	£ p	£ p	£ p	£ p	£ p	£ p	£ p	£ p	£ p
Totals										

Monthly Income Record

for the month of _____ 199___

	Date	A Description	B Bonuses & Product Sales		C Trainings & Events		D Misc. Income		E VAT Content		F Misc. Non-Vatable Income		G Gross Income (Total: cols B-F)		H Total Banked	
			£	p	£	p	£	p	£	p	£	p	£	p	£	
1																
2																
3																
4																
5																
6																
7																
8																
9																
10																
11																
12																
13																
14																
15																
16																
17																
18																
19																
20																
21																
22																
23																
24																
25																
26																
27																
28																
29																
30																
31																
32																
33																
34																
35																
36																
37																
38																
39																
40																
41																
42																
43																
44																
45																
46																
47																
48																
49																
50																
		Monthly Totals														

Monthly Expenditure Record

I	J		K		L		M		N		O		P		Q		R		S	
Method Ch#, Csh D/D, S/O	Petrol, Oil & Vehicle Service		Hotel, Travel & Subsistence		Admin. & Phone		Product & Samples		Misc. Expenditure		VAT Content		Postage		Misc. Non-Vatable Expenditure		Gross Expenditure (Total: cols J-Q)		Cumulative Running Total	
	£	p	£	p	£	p	£	p	£	p	£	p	£	p	£	p	£	p	£	p
Totals																				

Monthly Income Record

for the month of _____ **199___**

	A	B		C		D		E		F		G		H	
Date	Description	Bonuses & Product Sales		Trainings & Events		Misc. Income		VAT Content		Misc. Non-Vatable Income		Gross Income (Total: cols B-F)		Total Banked	
		£	p	£	p	£	p	£	p	£	p	£	p	£	p
1															
2															
3															
4															
5															
6															
7															
8															
9															
10															
11															
12															
13															
14															
15															
16															
17															
18															
19															
20															
21															
22															
23															
24															
25															
26															
27															
28															
29															
30															
31															
32															
33															
34															
35															
36															
37															
38															
39															
40															
41															
42															
43															
44															
45															
46															
47															
48															
49															
50															
	Monthly Totals														

Monthly Expenditure Record

	I	J		K		L		M		N		O		P		Q		R		S	
	Method Ch#, Csh D/D, S/O	Petrol, Oil & Vehicle Service		Hotel, Travel & Subsistence		Admin. & Phone		Product & Samples		Misc. Expenditure		VAT Content		Postage		Misc. Non-Vatable Expenditure		Gross Expenditure (Total: cols J-Q)		Cumulative Running Total	
		£	p	£	p	£	p	£	p	£	p	£	p	£	p	£	p	£	p	£	p
1																					
2																					
3																					
4																					
5																					
6																					
7																					
8																					
9																					
10																					
11																					
12																					
13																					
14																					
15																					
16																					
17																					
18																					
19																					
20																					
Totals																					

85

Monthly Income Record

for the month of _____ 199___

	A	B		C		D		E		F		G		H	
Date	Description	Bonuses & Product Sales		Trainings & Events		Misc. Income		VAT Content		Misc. Non-Vatable Income		Gross Income (Total: cols B-F)		Total Banked	
		£	p	£	p	£	p	£	p	£	p	£	p	£	p
1															
2															
3															
4															
5															
6															
7															
8															
9															
10															
11															
12															
13															
14															
15															
16															
17															
18															
19															
20															
21															
22															
23															
24															
25															
26															
27															
28															
29															
30															
31															
32															
33															
34															
35															
36															
37															
38															
39															
40															
41															
42															
43															
44															
45															
46															
47															
48															
49															
50															
	Monthly Totals														

Monthly Expenditure Record

	I	J		K		L		M		N		O		P		Q		R		S	
	Method Ch#, Csh D/D, S/O	Petrol, Oil & Vehicle Service		Hotel, Travel & Subsistence		Admin. & Phone		Product & Samples		Misc. Expenditure		VAT Content		Postage		Misc. Non- Vatable Expenditure		Gross Expenditure (Total: cols J-Q)		Cumulative Running Total	
		£	p	£	p	£	p	£	p	£	p	£	p	£	p	£	p	£	p	£	p
1																					
2																					
3																					
4																					
5																					
6																					
7																					
8																					
9																					
10																					
11																					
12																					
13																					
14																					
15																					
16																					
17																					
18																					
19																					
20																					
21																					
22																					
23																					
24																					
25																					
26																					
27																					
28																					
29																					
30																					
31																					
32																					
33																					
34																					
35																					
36																					
37																					
38																					
39																					
40																					
41																					
42																					
43																					
44																					
45																					
46																					
47																					
48																					
49																					
50																					
Totals																					

Monthly Income Record

for the month of _____ 199___

		A	B Bonuses & Product Sales		C Trainings & Events		D Misc. Income		E VAT Content		F Misc. Non-Vatable Income		G Gross Income (Total: cols B-F)		H Total Banked	
	Date	Description	£	p	£	p	£	p	£	p	£	p	£	p	£	p
1																
2																
3																
4																
5																
6																
7																
8																
9																
10																
11																
12																
13																
14																
15																
16																
17																
18																
19																
20																
21																
22																
23																
24																
25																
26																
27																
28																
29																
30																
31																
32																
33																
34																
35																
36																
37																
38																
39																
40																
41																
42																
43																
44																
45																
46																
47																
48																
49																
50																
		Monthly Totals														

Monthly Expenditure Record

I	J		K		L		M		N		O		P		Q		R		S	
Method Ch#, Csh D/D, S/O	Petrol, Oil & Vehicle Service		Hotel, Travel & Subsistence		Admin. & Phone		Product & Samples		Misc. Expenditure		VAT Content		Postage		Misc. Non-Vatable Expenditure		Gross Expenditure (Total: cols J-Q)		Cumulative Running Total	
	£	p	£	p	£	p	£	p	£	p	£	p	£	p	£	p	£	p	£	p
Totals																				

89

Monthly Income Record

for the month of _____ 199____

	Date	A Description	B Bonuses & Product Sales		C Trainings & Events		D Misc. Income		E VAT Content		F Misc. Non-Vatable Income		G Gross Income (Total: cols B-F)		H Total Banked	
			£	p	£	p	£	p	£	p	£	p	£	p	£	
1																
2																
3																
4																
5																
6																
7																
8																
9																
10																
11																
12																
13																
14																
15																
16																
17																
18																
19																
20																
21																
22																
23																
24																
25																
26																
27																
28																
29																
30																
31																
32																
33																
34																
35																
36																
37																
38																
39																
40																
41																
42																
43																
44																
45																
46																
47																
48																
49																
50																
		Monthly Totals														

Monthly Expenditure Record

I	J		K		L		M		N		O		P		Q		R		S	
Method Ch#, Csh D/D, S/O	Petrol, Oil & Vehicle Service		Hotel, Travel & Subsistence		Admin. & Phone		Product & Samples		Misc. Expenditure		VAT Content		Postage		Misc. Non-Vatable Expenditure		Gross Expenditure (Total: cols J-Q)		Cumulative Running Total	
	£	p	£	p	£	p	£	p	£	p	£	p	£	p	£	p	£	p	£	p
Totals																				

Cumulative Profit/Loss for the Year   199____

Month	Income	Expenditure	Profit/Loss	VAT on Income	VAT on Expenditure	VAT Due
1.						
2.						
Year to date:						
3.						
Year to date:						
4.						
Year to date:						
5.						
Year to date:						
6.						
Year to date:						
7.						
Year to date:						
8.						
Year to date:						
9.						
Year to date:						
10.						
Year to date:						
11.						
Year to date:						
12.						
Totals for year:						

Notes:

If you are not VAT registered, ignore the three right hand columns as they do not apply to you.

If you are VAT registered, exclude VAT from your entries in the three left-hand columns and enter your VAT totals in the right hand columns. The difference between VAT on Income and VAT on Expenditure is the sum of VAT Due. Use these figures to easily complete your VAT returns. You may have to add additional VAT for the use of your car.

Do You Want To Supercharge Your Business To Even More Success?

Then don't miss out on David Barber's S.T.A.R. Leadership Programme!

This is the most complete, workable and **EFFECTIVE** business building system in the industry. Here you will find a wealth of detailed advice about applying the ideas in *Target Success!* Just follow the Programme step-by-step from your first prospecting phone call to the most advanced leadership techniques. Build up your confidence, inject momentum into your business, and develop the downline leaders who will propel you to success!

The three books in the programme are:

- *Get Off To A Winning Start In Network Marketing (£8.99)*
- *Breakthrough Sponsoring & Retailing (£8.99)*
- *How To Lead A Winning Group (£9.99).*

And if you are looking to bring the power of personal development to your business, you will find down-to-earth answers in David Barber's *Network Marketeers... Supercharge Yourself!* (£8.99).

'Our distributors voted your books the best anywhere in the world—even better than the Americans'

Robin Forsyth (Corporate Manager)

'Should be a block-buster seller'

Tom 'Big Al' Schreiter (Network Marketing Legend)

'I was struggling until I read your books and attended your seminars—now my business is really taking off!'

B.L. (Distributor)

Please ask your book supplier for details.

 **SIGHT**
PUBLISHING

The UK's Premier Service
To The
Network Marketing Industry

Having difficulty finding the training resources and services you need?

We can help you with:

- Our all-new range of leading-edge British books and tapes featuring David Barber, Peter Clothier, Bruce King, Trevor Lowe, Derek Ross and more

- Exclusive distributor for leading US materials

- Bookings for training and motivational seminars, workshops and keynote speeches on: generating momentum; business-building; sponsoring, retailing; teaching; leadership; personal development

- Consultants to corporate teams and leading distributors

- Advice on setting up book distribution services, starter packs, distributor manuals, sales aids and the law relating to network marketing

- Writers and producers of recruiting and starter books, tapes and videos for companies and leading distributors.

For more information, just ring us on
01989-564496
or complete the form overleaf.

Yes!

Please send me regular news about books, tapes, events and training services from the Insight Network Marketing Library.

1st Name _____ (Mr/Mrs/Miss/Ms)

Last Name _____

Address _____

_____

Postcode _____ Phone _____ AM / PM / Evening

My network marketing company is _____

My group size is around _____ distributors.

I am especially interested in information on:

- Prospecting leaflets & booklets   Yes / No
- Materials for new distributors   Yes / No
- Effective sponsoring & retailing   Yes / No
- Self-development   Yes / No
- Phone counselling with David Barber   Yes / No
- Bookings with top trainers and speakers Yes / No
- Wholesale price arrangements   Yes / No

Customer feedback—please let us know what you think!

Any success stories or problems with applying the ideas in this book?

_____

_____

_____

_____

Did you like this book? Then please help us to spread the message by writing a few words recommending it to other distributors:

_____

_____

_____

_____

Can we use your comments on our publicity? *Yes* ☐ *Yes, with name disguised* ☐ *No* ☐

Please mail FREE to:
Insight Publishing
Freepost SWC0330
Ross-on-Wye
HR9 5BR

Or fax to 01989-565596

Thank You!